Illustrations copyright © 1992 by Julie Lacome.
All rights reserved. Published by Scholastic Inc., 555 Broadway,
New York, NY 10012, by arrangement with Candlewick Press.
Printed in the U.S.A.
ISBN 0-590-67895-7

2 3 4 5 6 7 8 9 10   08   02 01 00 99 98 97 96

by Edward Lear
illustrated by Julie Lacome

SCHOLASTIC INC.

New York   Toronto   London   Auckland   Sydney

A was once an apple pie,
Pidy
Widy
Tidy
Pidy
Nice insidy
Apple pie.

B was once a little bear,

Beary

Wary

Hairy

Beary

Taky cary

Little bear.

3

Cc

C was once a little cake,
Caky
Baky
Maky
Caky
Taky caky
Little cake.

D was once a little doll,
Dolly
Molly
Polly
Nolly
Nursy dolly
Little doll.

E was once a little eel,
Eely
Weely
Peely
Eely
Twirly tweely
Little eel.

Ff

F was once a little fish,
Fishy
Wishy
Squishy
Fishy
In a dishy
Little fish.

Gg

G was once a little goose,
Goosy
Moosy
Boosey
Goosey
Waddly woosy
Little goose.

H was once a little hen,
Henny
Chenny
Tenny
Henny
Eggsy any
Little hen?

I was once a bottle of ink,
Inky
Dinky
Thinky
Inky
Blacky minky
Bottle of ink.

J was once a jar of jam,
Jammy
Mammy
Clammy
Jammy
Sweety swammy
Jar of jam.

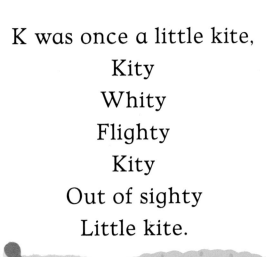

Kk

K was once a little kite,
Kity
Whity
Flighty
Kity
Out of sighty
Little kite.

L l

L was once a little lark,
Larky
Marky
Harky
Larky
In the parky
Little lark.

Mm

M was once a little mouse,
Mousey
Bousey
Sousy
Mousy
In the housy
Little mouse.

13

14

N was once a little needle,
Needly
Tweedly
Threedly
Needly
Wisky wheedly
Little needle.

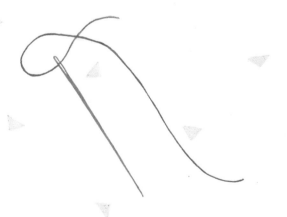

O was once a little owl,

Owly

Prowly

Howly

Owly

Browny fowly

Little owl.

Pp

P was once a little pump,
Pumpy
Slumpy
Flumpy
Pumpy
Dumpy thumpy
Little pump.

Qq

Q was once a little quail,
Quaily
Faily
Daily
Quaily
Stumpy taily
Little quail.

Rr

R was once a little rose,
Rosy
Posy
Nosy
Rosy
Blows-y grows-y
Little rose.

S was once a little shrimp,
  Shrimpy
  Nimpy
  Flimpy
  Shrimpy
  Jumpy jimpy
  Little shrimp.

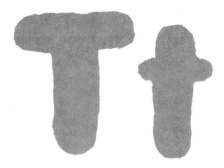

T was once a little thrush,
  Thrushy
  Hushy
  Bushy
  Thrushy
  Flitty flushy
  Little thrush.

U was once a little urn,
Urny
Burny
Turny
Urny
Bubbly burny
Little urn.

URN

V was once a little vine,
Viny
Winy
Twiny
Viny
Twisty twiny
Little vine.

W was once a whale,
Whaly
Scaly
Shaly
Whaly
Tumbly taily
Mighty whale.

23

X was once a great King Xerxes,
Xerxy
Perxy
Turxy
Xerxy
Linxy Lurxy
Great King Xerxes.

Y was once a little yew,
    Yewdy
    Fewdy
    Crudy
    Yewdy
  Growdy grewdy
    Little yew.

ZINC

Z was once a piece of zinc,
    Tinky
    Winky
    Blinky
    Tinky
  Tinkly minky
  Piece of zinc.

THE COMPASSIONATE CHICK's GUIDE to DIY BEAUTY

125 RECIPES for Vegan, Gluten-Free, Cruelty-Free Makeup, Skin & Hair Products

Sunny Subramanian
veganbeautyreview.com
& Chrystle Fiedler

Robert
ROSE

For complete cataloguing information, see page 272.

Disclaimer
The author and the publisher are not responsible for any adverse effects or consequences resulting from the use of the information in this book. It is the responsibility of the reader to consult a physician or other qualified health-care professional regarding his or her personal care.

To the best of our knowledge, the recipes or formulas in this book are safe for ordinary use and users. For those people with allergies or health issues, please read the suggested contents of each recipe or formula carefully and determine whether or not they may create a problem for you. All recipes or formulas are used at the risk of the consumer.

We cannot be responsible for any hazards, loss or damage that may occur as a result of any recipe or formula use.

For those with special needs, allergies, requirements or health problems, in the event of any doubt, please contact your medical adviser prior to the use of any recipe or formula.

Design and Production: Daniella Zanchetta/PageWave Graphics Inc.
Editor: Tina Anson Mine
Copyeditor/proofreader: Marnie Lamb
Indexer: Beth Zabloski
Photography & Prop Styling: Michelle Cehn *(except as noted below)*
Recipe Preparation & Styling: Sunny Subramanian
Assistant to Sunny: Kari Repsholdt

Additional images: p.1 Baby rabbit © iStockphoto.com/Burcin Tolga Kural; p.7 Pink sky clouds © iStockphoto.com/Shadowalice; Pink origami butterflies © iStockphoto.com/Ekaart; Circles © iStockphoto.com/Oksana Pasishnychenko; Feathers © iStockphoto.com/Marina Zakharova; p.14 Rabbit pattern © iStockphoto.com/Embra; Orange diamonds © iStockphoto.com/Tiax; p.17 Pink floral © iStockphoto.com/Anastasiya Yatchenko; Light blue pattern © iStockphoto.com/Tiax; p.21 Rabbit © iStockphoto.com/Chenyuzheng; p.27 Pink diamonds pattern © iStockphoto.com/Pulvas; Blue & yellow pattern © iStockphoto.com/Tiax; p.33 Pomegranate © iStockphoto.com/Mashuk; p.39 Teal & gray pattern © iStockphoto.com/Tiax; Yellow butterflies © iStockphoto.com/Aleksa; p.45 Jojoba © iStockphoto.com/Mashuk; p.53 Rosemary essential oil © iStockphoto.com/Christopher Ames; p.54 Orange essential oil © iStockphoto.com/Elena Gaak; p.55 Bergamot © iStockphoto.com/Aon_Skynotlimit; p.57 Dropper into bottle © iStockphoto.com/MorePixels; p.58 Cherry pattern © iStockphoto.com/Naddiya; Floral bird pattern © iStockphoto.com/Embra; p.61 Purple birds © iStockphoto.com/Oksancia; Mint waves © iStockphoto.com/Tiax; p.79 Lemons © iStockphoto.com/Julichka; p.121 Bananas © iStockphoto.com/Kauriana; Scallops © iStockphoto.com/Kidstudio852; p.153 Essential oils © iStockphoto.com/Botamochi; p.171 Hops © iStockphoto.com/Richard Loader; p.173 Green dotted © iStockphoto.com/AlenaZ0509; Triangles © iStockphoto.com/Kidstudio852; p.199 Floral & bird pattern © iStockphoto.com/Nataliia Kucherencko; Orange geometric © iStockphoto.com/Tukkki; p.227 Blue diamond flower pattern © iStockphoto.com/Tiax; Circular flowers © iStockphoto.com/Embra; p.251 Pink lollipops © iStockphoto.com/Maria Tkach; Red lollipops © iStockphoto.com/Maria Tkach; p.257 Nail polish bottles © iStockphoto.com/Nik Merkulov

The publisher gratefully acknowledges the financial support of our publishing program by the Government of Canada through the Canada Book Fund.

Published by Robert Rose Inc.
120 Eglinton Avenue East, Suite 800, Toronto, Ontario, Canada M4P 1E2
Tel: (416) 322-6552 Fax: (416) 322-6936
www.robertrose.ca

Printed and bound in Canada

1 2 3 4 5 6 7 8 9 TCP 24 23 22 21 20 19 18 17 16

Contents

Acknowledgments...7
Introduction..9
How to Use This Book..12

Part One: The Ins and Outs of Vegan Beauty.......15
Chapter 1: Vegan Basics.....................................17
Chapter 2: Why DIY Beauty Products Are Better...............27
Chapter 3: Essential Vegan Ingredients and Equipment.......39

Part Two: The Recipes...........................59
Chapter 4: Face Care..61
Chapter 5: Bath and Body Care..............................121
Chapter 6: Hair Care.......................................173
Chapter 7: Makeup and Cosmetics............................199
Chapter 8: Unisex Beauty Essentials........................227

APPENDICES.....................................251
- Appendix A: Favorite Natural, Organic Ingredients
  and What They Do...252
- Appendix B: Favorite All-Natural, Vegan-Friendly
  Beauty Brands..254
- Appendix C: DIY Beauty Routines: Looking Gorgeous
  from Morning to Night....................................258
- Appendix D: Tips for Labeling, Packaging and
  Giving DIY Vegan Beauty Products.........................261

RESOURCES......................................262
- The Best Places to Shop for Ingredients,
  Tools and Supplies.......................................262
- Resources for Vegan Living and Vegan Beauty.............264

Index...265

Acknowledgments

I dedicate this book with a huge, heaping loaf of love to my incredible, sweet and loving hubby, Avi; my two kiddos, Dylan and Devendra; my mom; and my fur babies Spirulina and Conan (and Towane, who has passed but lives forever in our hearts). Also, I'd like to say a huge thank-you to my family, friends and the supporters of Vegan Beauty Review, who have been a huge inspiration and motivating force for me every single day.

— Sunny Subramanian

Many thanks to Sunny for her vibrant expression of vegan living and love of animals, to Marilyn Allen for being an indefatigable and wise agent, to Tina Anson Mine for her thoughtful and precise editing, and to Bob Dees and the entire team at Robert Rose Publishing.

My late beloved dachshund Holmes, forever missed; my dachshund rescues Wallander and Murdoch; and my cats, Tinker and Tuppence, also rescues, all inspired me. For them, I dedicate this book to all of the organizations that work tirelessly to end animal cruelty, and to improve the health, welfare and well-being of domestic, farm and wild animals. You help make the world a more humane and hopeful place to live. Thank you.

— Chrystle Fiedler

Introduction

So who is this chick concocting vegan beauty recipes in her kitchen? Hello! My name is Sunny, and I'm a compassionate vegan beauty junkie who likes to stir up DIY magic in the kitchen.

I've had the most gigantic, gooshiest soft spot for animals my whole life. (Seriously, I was destined to be a crazy cat lady by age two.) In April 2000, during a college philosophy course focused on ethics, I watched footage of undercover animal cruelty investigations conducted by People for the Ethical Treatment of Animals (PETA) and had the biggest Oprah-style "Aha!" moment. I thought, "Hold up. I love animals … but I eat them?" I went vegan in a heartbeat; I didn't even go through a vegetarian phase. Once you know something, you can't unknow it, you know?

I had my fur babies (over the years, Towane, Spirulina and Conan have been my beloved fluff muffins), but I realized that all animals — cows, lambs, pigs, turkeys, chickens and even creepy crawlies — could be my homies if I just got to know them. Life is precious, and we're all sentient beings who think and feel.

After that, my mindset completely shifted. Overnight, I became a vegan because I love animals. My philosophy is that I never want to contribute to the pain and suffering of any living being.

Awareness into Action

Once my eyes were opened, I ditched meat, fish, dairy, eggs, honey and all other animal products from my diet. I began scrupulously reading ingredient labels on everything — and I mean everything. If I spotted some grody animal ingredient like casein, a protein found in mammals' milk, I'd think to myself, "Oh, hell no!" That meant putting a lot of scrumptious-looking nonvegan cookies back on the shelf. Call me crazy, but bovine mammary secretions don't really sound appetizing to me.

Today, there are a plethora of vegan options right on regular grocery store shelves. But back in 2000, that wasn't the case. This lack of alternatives required me to step out of my comfort zone and exercise plenty of self-control. Seriously, folks, putting cookies back on a shelf does *not* come naturally to me.

My Beauty Vegucation

After my revelation, it didn't take long to realize that I'd have to completely reboot my lifestyle. Going vegan meant I had to ditch animal by-products entirely. I'd have to reeducate myself on food, beauty, fashion, everything! So, just like I had done with my groceries, I became a diligent reader of beauty-product labels.

All of a sudden, some of my favorite beauty brands no longer made the grade, because I discovered they were tested on animals or contained animal-derived ingredients. Others were vegan and cruelty-free but still contained unhealthy chemicals. Some of the products in my beauty regimen were made with synthetic ingredients that had names so long I couldn't pronounce them if I tried.

Having set a new, higher bar for the products I was willing to use, I began to search online for vegan beauty suggestions and product raves to guide me in my choices. I didn't have much luck. That's when I realized there was a void that needed to be filled. There were people out there like me, who wanted to enhance their beauty naturally without causing suffering to animals. They needed a go-to resource. And, just like that, my mission became clear. I got down to business, happily gathering information to share with the world. And that, ladies and germs, is how my baby was born. I launched Vegan Beauty Review (www.veganbeautyreview.com) as a blog in 2007, and built my presence as a cruelty-free advocate across social media.

So What's Vegan Beauty Review?

Vegan Beauty Review (VBR) is an online hub that provides savvy consumers with sparkly, entertaining, cruelty-free beauty tips and inspo. It offers up vegan, organic and eco-friendly product reviews covering animal-friendly fashion and vegan food, and DIY beauty recipes. I feature the best of the best for my growing audience of fellow cruelty-free beauty babes. My main goal is to show veg-curious peeps that vegan beauty can be girlie and fun while still being responsible.

After I started VBR, the vegan beauty scene exploded. I used to be familiar with almost every single beauty brand back when I started blogging in 2007, but today, it's a (very positive) challenge to keep up. There are cruelty-free beauty lines popping up every single day. Vegan products are more accessible than ever, even at drugstores and chain stores, such as Target and Sephora.

I'm simply obsessed with finding and sharing info on the most effective cruelty-free beauty products. I want everyone to enjoy the best facial masks, body scrubs, eye creams, cleansers, toners and makeup — all made with the purest ingredients and sans the ick factor (nasty chemicals, additives and preservatives). These products have to be absolutely free of animal products and developed without any cruel animal testing.

Why DIY Is the Best

Through my work on VBR, I became mega-familiar with the ingredients used in my favorite beauty products. This inspired me to try my hand at stirring up my own recipes from scratch. I noticed that many of my go-to skin-care products contained natural oils (such as avocado, grapeseed and olive), sugars, salts, citrus juices, extracts, herbs and spices — all ingredients that were just chilling out in my kitchen. Once I made the connection, I decided it was time to play.

Most whole foods are nutrient-dense with lots of skin-loving properties. This makes them the perfect addition to your grooming routine. Besides being convenient, fun and budget-friendly, making beauty products from scratch means you have complete control over what goes on your skin.

I've whipped up some highly effective recipes that have saved my skin time and time again. They've helped out with bouts of hormonal acne; insanely flaky, dry, wintery skin; and the dreaded arrival of fine lines and wrinkles. It's a joy experimenting with ingredients and finding combos that work in perfect harmony. I've also adapted and tweaked timeless DIY recipes, some of which have been handed down to me by my beautiful mama, who runs an Etsy store that sells vegan skin-care products. My mama taught me many of my favorite techniques, which I'm passing on to you, from using cornstarch as a dry shampoo to moisturizing your hair with natural oils.

My DIY beauty recipes, tutorials, tips and tricks have become increasingly popular on VBR, so I thought it made sense to compile them in this book so you have a go-to resource. I'm so happy to share my innovative beauty solutions with you. I hope it will empower you to take matters into your own hands and DIY it up, making products from scratch that are nourishing, potent and effective.

— Sunny Subramanian

How to Use This Book

This book is a natural outgrowth of my successful blog, Vegan Beauty Review (www.veganbeautyreview.com), and a fun, empowering resource that will show you how to make your own vegan beauty products. The book is divided into two sections.

You can jump right into the recipes in Part Two, or read Part One first so you have a better idea of the value DIY beauty offers you and the planet. Either way, you'll have fun and do your part to end animal cruelty, making the world a better place while looking gorgeous.

Part One: The Ins and Outs of Vegan Beauty

This section of the book is all about education and preparation. It covers all the background you need to get you ready to make the recipes in Part Two.

- **Chapter 1:** Here, I'll give you the details on what being a vegan means. I'll cover strategies for making the switch to a vegan lifestyle, and the differences between the terms *vegan* and *cruelty-free*. You'll learn why it's important to use only products that haven't been tested on animals, and ones that don't contain animal ingredients or by-products.

- **Chapter 2:** Next up, you'll discover the many benefits of making your own vegan makeup and beauty products. You'll find out about the dangers of some common toxins that are in store-bought cosmetics and body-care potions, and learn how to avoid them. You'll discover that DIY-ing saves you money, and is kind to the Earth and good for the soul. I'll share with you the positive impact your vegan lifestyle will have on animal welfare, and show you why making your own beauty stuff is fun, fun, fun! I'll even give you some hints on clearing out your old beauty products to make room for your new ones.

- **Chapter 3:** Last, we'll explore the ingredients and supplies you'll need to have on hand to take on Part Two of this book. I'll also give you some storage recommendations and safety tips that will keep you (and your DIY beauty products) in top condition.

Part Two: The Recipes

This section of the book gives you 125 vegan, gluten-free recipes that cover all of the major beauty-product categories: face and hair care, bath and body products, makeup, and grooming essentials including toothpaste and deodorant. Each recipe will give you step-by-step instructions and help you bring out your beauty naturally.

Along with each recipe, you'll find interesting, illuminating and useful info. Look for the following categories:

TOP TİP: What you need to know about the recipe, an alternative use for an ingredient or the formula itself, or a helpful piece of advice.

★ **Superstar ingredient:** The goods on an ingredient that deserves special attention, due to its amazing properties for face, skin, hair, body or overall well-being.

DID YOU KNOW?: Interesting tidbits or thought-provoking background information about an ingredient or bodily process.

Caution: A note that tells you to take special care with a particular ingredient.

Skin-Care Symbol Legend

It's time to get busy in the kitchen and get your natural beauty on! But wait. Before you do, check out the symbols on the right. As you go through Part Two, you'll see them scattered across my recipes. They'll help point you in the direction of solutions that are right for your skin or hair type.

Best for:

♥ All skin/hair types
● Normal skin/hair
◐ Combination skin
◉ Oily/acne-prone skin/oily hair
▲ Dry skin/hair
✳ Dandruff-prone hair
≋ Thinning/brittle hair
◆ Sensitive skin
■ Mature skin

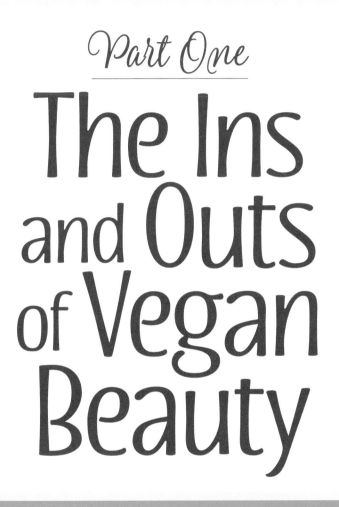

Part One

The Ins and Outs of Vegan Beauty

Chapter 1

Vegan Basics

Vegetarians don't eat meat, poultry or fish, while vegans, like me, take it a step further. Vegans don't consume any animal products or by-products. That means we avoid meat, poultry and fish like vegetarians, *plus* eggs, dairy products, honey, leather, fur, silk and wool. Anything a vegan eats or uses doesn't come from animals, so this makes the lifestyle naturally cruelty-free.

There's a popular myth that vegans can eat only soybeans and salad. But that couldn't be further from the truth. In real life, vegans eat everything nonvegans eat. Just hold the animal products or by-products. Trust me, I still get my fair share of pasta, burritos, pizza, sushi, burgers, egg-free scrambles, ice cream, cake and all that jazz. It just comes sans the flesh, cow juice and chicken periods. Whoops, did I just tell it like it is? Yep, I did.

Plant-based foods are where it's at, y'all. And if you've got a hankering for chicken, beef or even crab, you can totally rock the faux versions available at the grocery store. There are tons of popular brands, including Gardein, Beyond Meat, Tofurky, Boca, Lightlife, Yves Veggie Cuisine, Field Roast and Gardenburger. Jonesing for cheese? Try dairy-free brands, such as Daiya, Follow Your Heart, Kite Hill, Miyoko's Kitchen, Dr. Cow, Tofutti, Treeline Treenut Cheese, Vtopian Artisan Cheeses, Heidi Ho and Field Roast Chao cheeses. When you get all those groceries home, there are lots of recipes for them on my blog.

Vegucational Films
To learn more about why it's important to go vegan, check out these important and illuminating flicks:

- *The Cove*
- *Cowspiracy*
- *Earthlings*
- *Fat, Sick & Nearly Dead*
- *Food, Inc.*
- *Food Matters*
- *Forks over Knives* (you may see a familiar face at the end — wink!)
- *Hungry for Change*
- *Peaceable Kingdom*
- *Super Size Me*
- *Vegucated*

People Are Going Vegan — Big-Time

Veganism is on the rise. More and more people are discovering the links between meat consumption and their health, and they are concerned about animal welfare and the meat industry's environmental impact. According to a 2012 Harris Interactive poll commissioned by the Vegetarian Resource Group, the number of people who eat a plant-based diet makes up a significant segment of the population. Out of the approximately 240 million U.S. adults aged 18 and older, 8 million are consciously and compassionately choosing to be vegetarians, and 1 million of those vegetarians are vegans.

Canadians are even more enthusiastic about going meat-free. According to a 2015 poll commissioned by the Vancouver Humane Society, 33% of Canadians (almost 12 million people) are now making compassionate choices. Of this figure, 8% identify as vegetarian or mostly vegetarian, and the remaining 25% are making a conscious effort to eat less meat.

Interested in becoming a vegan? Get a free vegan starter kit from PETA at www.peta.org, and one from the Physicians Committee for Responsible Medicine at www.pcrm.org.

Farm Sanctuary

Farm Sanctuary was founded in 1986 to help protect animals, such as cows, pigs, chickens and goats, from the abusive factory farming system. Today, Farm Sanctuary works to raise awareness, end cruel practices, and rescue and place animals in sanctuaries in Watkins Glen, New York; Orland, California; and Los Angeles, California. As Farm Sanctuary likes to say, animals are friends, not food.

In 2015, actor-comedian Jon Stewart and his wife, Tracey, began a partnership with Farm Sanctuary, and will open a new branch of this rescue organization in New Jersey. Tracey has also written a wonderful book to help raise awareness about people's treatment of animals. It's called *Do unto Animals: A Friendly Guide to how Animals Live, and how We Can Make Their Lives Better* (Artisan, 2015). Bonus: when you buy it, part of the proceeds go to benefit Farm Sanctuary.

Want to learn more about Farm Sanctuary and how you can make a difference? Pick up a copy of *Living the Farm Sanctuary Life: The Ultimate Guide to Eating Mindfully, Living Longer, and Feeling Better Every Day* (Rodale, 2015) by cofounder Gene Baur. And make sure you check out the website, www.farmsanctuary.org.

Why I Believe in DIY Vegan Beauty

You've heard time and time again that you are what you eat. But did you know that what you put *on* your body is just as important as what you put *in* your body?

Skin, the body's largest organ, absorbs up to 60% of everything you put on it. I try not to put anything on my skin that I wouldn't put in my mouth, and that means most everything I use is vegan, organic and super-healthy.

Using DIY vegan beauty products means I know exactly what I'm putting on my face, hair and body. I moisturize with sweet almond and coconut oils, scrub my skin and lips with brown sugar and coconut oil, steam my face over my teapot filled with fresh herbs, and take baths in nut milks and natural salts.

Click for More Info
My website, VBR (www.veganbeautyreview.com), has an extensive and frequently updated list of cruelty-free and vegan-friendly beauty brands. Check it out for up-to-date intel.

When you opt to buy most conventional beauty products available in the marketplace, you're often paying for hyped-up, overpriced, chemical-laden crap. Plus, many of these products contain harmful, dangerous toxins and have been tested on innocent animals. Ugh.

Toxins in Makeup and Beauty Products

You may find it hard to believe, but cosmetic companies can pretty much do whatever they want. They can use just about any ingredient or raw material in their products, except for certain color additives and a few prohibited substances.

You've seen the long lists of ingredients on your personal-care products. But did you know that there are more than 82,000 of them, and that one in eight are carcinogens, pesticides, reproductive toxins and hormone disrupters? But that's not all: products often contain plasticizers, the chemicals that keep concrete soft so it can be poured; degreasers, which are used in garages to clean auto parts; and surfactants, which help reduce surface tension in dyes. Think about what these harsh chemicals do to your skin and to our world.

Many popular beauty brands contain nasty chemicals, such as butylated hydroxyanisole (BHA), butylated hydroxytoluene (BHT), diethanolamine (DEA), petroleum, siloxanes, formaldehyde and sodium laureth sulfate. Some are known or suspected carcinogens, meaning they can cause cancer; others are toxins that interfere with brain, reproductive and endocrine functions. If you're using products that contain these ingredients, you're putting yourself at risk. That's why I'm so passionate about making my own makeup and beauty treatments, and helping you do the same.

Animal Testing Is Cruel, Unnecessary and Inaccurate

You'd think that animal testing would be a thing of the past in the progressive world we live in. Sadly, it isn't. In the United States, a large percentage of the animals used in animal testing receive absolutely no protection under the *Animal Welfare Act*.

Researchers and scientists at cosmetic companies routinely abuse mice, rats, guinea pigs and rabbits as they test their beauty products before going to market. Unfortunately, several animal tests are common practice during beauty-product development. According to the Humane Society of the United States, these include the following:

- Skin and eye irritation tests, in which chemicals are rubbed onto the shaved skin or dripped into the eyes of restrained rabbits that have not received any pain-killers.

- Repeated force-feeding studies lasting for weeks or months, in which animals are made to ingest a substance so testers can look for signs of general illness or specific health hazards, such as cancer or birth defects.

- "Lethal dose" tests, in which animals are forced to swallow large amounts of a test chemical to determine the dose that causes them to die. This practice has been widely condemned by the public, but it still happens.

At the end of a test, the animals are killed, normally by asphyxiation, neck breaking or decapitation. Pain relief is not provided. Horrifying, isn't it?

We all want to look and feel our best, but it should never be at the expense of innocent animals' suffering.

Animal Testing and the Law

It's important to know that in the United States animal testing is *not* required by law. Neither the U.S. Food and Drug Administration (FDA) nor the U.S. Consumer Product Safety Commission requires companies to test cosmetics or household products on animals.

In fact, the FDA supports alternatives to animal testing! Its website, www.fda.gov, states this very clearly on the Animal Testing & Cosmetics page in the Cosmetics section of the site: "FDA supports the development and use of alternatives to whole-animal testing as well as adherence to the most humane methods available within the limits of scientific capability when animals are used for testing the safety of cosmetic products. We will continue to be a strong advocate of methodologies for the refinement, reduction, and replacement of animal tests with alternative methodologies that do not employ the use of animals."

On the other hand, there are countries that still require animal testing. All cosmetics imported to China (and many that are made in that country), by law, must be tested on animals before entering the market. So even if an American or Canadian cosmetics company wanted to sell cruelty-free products in China, those products could no longer be considered cruelty-free after complying with this regulation.

Why Unscrupulous Companies Still Conduct Animal Testing

There are a couple of different motivations at work here. Sometimes, companies choose to develop or use new, untested ingredients in their products. They conduct tests on animals because they think the results will prove that the ingredients are safe for human use. Other companies test on animals because they want to brag about the unique beneficial properties of specific ingredients and need data to back up their claims.

Here's why this is so misguided. Animal tests are unreliable and ineffective — after all, they're testing human products on nonhuman species! According to the Humane Society of the United States, this means that consumer safety simply isn't guaranteed. The results are variable and difficult to interpret, which means the data really doesn't apply to humans, in the end. All those animals are killed, maimed and tortured for findings that just don't help make beauty products any safer. Unfortunately, companies will still test on animals as long as the demand for mainstream beauty products and makeup continues.

Alternatives to Animal Testing Are Out There

But wait — there is hope! Nonanimal testing can be — and is — done by companies that want to provide cruelty-free products. These alternatives smartly combine human cell–based studies and sophisticated computer models to deliver human-relevant results in hours or days. This not only speeds up the testing process considerably, but also saves animals from a terrible fate. Certainly, these options are so much better than inflicting pain on innocent creatures for months or years at a time, and then killing them using cruel methods.

Cruelty-Free vs. Vegan

Next, let's clear up any confusion about *cruelty-free* vs. *vegan*. You may need a little refresher on what these terms mean in the world of beauty products — and how they are not necessarily interchangeable.

Bottom line: cruelty-free products are *not* always vegan. By the same token, *accidentally vegan* products (see box, at right) are not always cruelty-free. *Cruelty-free* refers to products (and ingredients in products) that are not tested on animals, while *vegan* refers to ones that do not contain any animal-derived ingredients. I hope that, one day, *cruelty-free* will actually mean 100% cruelty-free — that is, zero animal testing and zero animal by-products.

What's *Accidentally Vegan*?
If someone sets out to make a vegan beauty product, it's logical that it would also be cruelty-free. However, there are accidentally vegan beauty products out there that aren't created intentionally to be marketed as vegan. They just happen to not have animal ingredients in them. That doesn't necessarily mean they haven't been tested on animals.

What Animal Products Really Are

Animal ingredients are not only cruel but also super-gross! Here are just a few examples of the nasty stuff that can end up in your cosmetic products under a more pleasant name:

- Allantoin (cow pee)
- Ambergris (whale barf)
- Beeswax and honey (bee barf)
- Carmine, or cochineal (crushed bugs)
- Castoreum (beaver scent gland juice)
- Civet (civet cat anal gland juice)
- Collagen (bones and sinews, or placenta)
- Elastin (cow neck ligaments and aortas)
- Lanolin (wool grease)
- Squalene (shark liver oil)
- Tallow (animal fat)

Blech, disgusting! I'm not cray for *not* wanting pee in my makeup — am I right or am I right? Toxins, animal cruelty and animal by-products are plenty of reasons why we're gonna take matters into our own hands and DIY it up.

Your Homework Assignment
There's a looooong list of ingredients in cosmetics, food and other things that may be derived from animals. They hide under a lot of different names. If you're concerned and want to bone up on these terms (pun intended), visit www.peta.org and check out their animal ingredients list. It's a terrific place to catch up on some vegan homework.

One Solution: Shop Cruelty-Free

PETA also has some fab cruelty-free shopping resources. If you visit www.peta.org and click on the Shop tab, you'll find a link to free super-handy resource lists of companies that do and don't conduct animal tests.

When you're shopping, be on the lookout for the words "Not tested on animals" on everything you buy. As well, look for the Leaping Bunny and PETA's cruelty-free bunny on packages. These logos are given to companies that comply with strict cruelty-free standards. Not all cruelty-free beauty brands use these logos; if you're in doubt about the status of a product, e-mail or call the company directly and ask questions such as these:

1. Does your company or manufacturer test on animals?

2. Do any third parties engage in animal testing on your behalf?

3. Do you use ingredients from suppliers that have tested their products on animals?

4. Do you sell products in China or any foreign market that requires animal testing?

Know a Company's Roots Before You Buy

It's important to note that some vegan and cruelty-free companies are actually owned by a parent company that conducts animal testing on other brands under its umbrella. Ugh. I know — there are so many variables to look out for! One example of this is Urban Decay. It is a cruelty-free beauty brand, but in 2012, it was acquired by L'Oréal, a mega-company that does animal testing where it's required by law (such as in China). Another example is cruelty-free Burt's Bees, which was purchased by Clorox, a huge corporation that routinely tests products on animals.

It's up to you to decide if these companies are worth supporting. Some would argue that supporting cruelty-free brands owned by parent companies that conduct animal tests ultimately supports more animal testing. Others would argue that any support of cruelty-free brands sends a message to the parent company, and the beauty market in general, that there is a growing demand for animal-friendly alternatives. The choice is yours to make.

Skip the Guilt Trip
I want to point out that you shouldn't beat yourself up if you've been buying cruelty-free products only to discover, after the fact, that they have animal ingredients in them. Nobody's perfect. Just like you, I'm a work in progress and, quite honestly, some ingredients are so ambiguous (with their 14-syllable scientific names) that it's virtually impossible to know exactly what you're buying. And that's why making your own products trumps all this craziness. Just head over to Chapter 2 for more reasons to get busy making your own DIY vegan beauty products.

Why DIY Beauty Products Are Better

In this chapter, you'll discover seven kick-ass benefits you'll get by ditching conventional cosmetics and beauty products, and making your own the vegan way. Not only will you be safer from the awful toxic gunk found in store-bought stuff, but you'll also help protect bunnies, improve the welfare of all furry creatures, save a significant amount of cash and have hella fun doing it!

Toxic Crap Out, Wholesome Beauty In

Y'all, check it: every day, the average woman uses a dozen products containing 168 different ingredients, many of which include phthalates (plasticizers), parabens (preservatives) and artificial fragrances. Really, it's hard to avoid them. According to the Environmental Working Group (EWG), the most-trusted authority on safe ingredients and consumer products, the majority of mainstream beauty brands contain chemicals, many of which are toxins. Does that give anybody else heart palpitations?

The Bad Stuff

For a real wake-up call, go to your bathroom. Right now. (I'll wait.) Grab a few of the products you use regularly, and check the labels for the following nasties:

- **BHA** and **BHT:** The National Toxicology Program, which is run by the National Institutes of Health in the United States, says BHA is "reasonably anticipated to be a human carcinogen." Scary stuff! It is also an endocrine disruptor. BHT is a cousin with similar issues.

- **Coal tar dyes:** A variety of these are banned in Europe and Canada, while others are still allowed for use in cosmetics, especially hair dyes. Coal tar dyes are a by-product of coal processing. They're a known carcinogen, according to the National Toxicology Program.

- **DEA** and **triethanolamine (TEA):** When these lather-creating substances react with other ingredients in cosmetics, they create carcinogenic compounds called nitrosamines, which have been linked to liver, stomach, bladder and esophageal cancers.

- **Dibutyl phthalate (DBP):** This fragrance ingredient and plasticizer is toxic to the reproductive system and an endocrine disruptor.

- **DMDM hydantoin** and **imidazolidinyl urea:** These antimicrobial preservatives are known allergens. They release formaldehyde (see below) to preserve commercial cosmetics.

- **Formaldehyde:** A potent preservative sometimes found in shampoo, conditioner, hair straighteners, skin moisturizers and nail polish, formaldehyde is a known carcinogen, allergen and irritant. Dude, they use this stuff to embalm dead bodies. And it stinks!

- **Hydroquinone:** This skin-bleaching chemical is used in lots of under-eye and whitening creams; it's also used to treat hyperpigmentation, acne scars, sun spots and other discolorations. Hydroquinone can cause a skin disease called ochronosis, which creates blue-black discolored patches of skin. In the worst cases, the patches become permanent, black, caviar-size bumps. Um, can we say nightmare material?

- **Lead:** You'll find this neurotoxin in the male hair dye Grecian Formula and some black dyes. But just because it goes on your head doesn't mean it stays there. Lead from black hair dye is dangerous because it can get on surfaces, where kids can ingest it.

- **Methylisothiazolinone (MI):** Considered a "safe" preservative alternative to parabens, it's a known skin irritant and allergen. Studies have also shown it to be a neurotoxin that is linked to brain cell and nerve damage.

- **Nanoparticles:** These incredibly tiny particles are often found in sprays and powders, and they can penetrate your lungs, enter your bloodstream and contaminate your body. Despite this effective and alarming delivery system for toxins, very little testing has been done on nanoparticles. No surprise: cosmetics manufacturers don't have to tell you that nanoparticles are in any of their products.

- **Oxybenzone:** According to the U.S. Centers for Disease Control and Prevention (CDC), this toxin found in sunscreens is present in just about every person's body. Research shows that oxybenzone causes irritation, allergies and disruption of the hormone system. Even more terrifying: it is associated with weight differences in newborn babies. Women who had higher concentrations of oxybenzone in their bodies had baby girls who weighed less and baby boys who weighed more than average.

- **Parabens:** These estrogen-mimicking preservatives — including propylparaben, isopropylparaben, butylparaben and isobutylparaben — can be found in most conventional cosmetics and skin-care products. They are used to extend a product's shelf life by hindering bacterial growth. Unfortunately, these carcinogens also disrupt the endocrine system and cause reproductive and developmental disorders in children. According to the CDC, nearly all Americans have parabens in their bodies.

- **Parfum (fragrance):** A study by the EWG and the Campaign for Safe Cosmetics found an average of 14 chemicals in 17 name-brand fragrance products — and not one was named on the label. Companies aren't required by U.S. federal law to list any of the chemicals in their fragrance formulas, because they are proprietary. Lame, right? Fragrances, which can be in almost anything from face cream to shampoo, can contain hormone disruptors and are some of the worst allergens. Some chemicals in fragrance are known carcinogens or neurotoxins. That's why I'm all about scenting my beauty products with pure, all-natural essential oils.

- **Petroleum by-products:** Often found in cosmetics like mascara, these ingredients include butylene glycol; dipropylene glycol; di-, tri- and tetrasodium ethylenediaminetetraacetic acid (EDTA); mineral oil; paraffin; petrolatum; polybutylene; polyethylene; and triclosan. They interfere with the skin's natural functioning, clog pores (read: cause zits!), cause contact dermatitis and can be contaminated with carcinogens that are implicated in cases of breast cancer.

- **Phthalates:** These chemicals help lotions penetrate your skin. They're also common ingredients in nail polish (making manis especially dangerous for pregnant women, because phthalates are linked to neurodevelopmental issues in babies). They're also frequently found in perfumes and products that have *fragrance* listed in the ingredients. Researchers have found links between phthalates and asthma, type 2 diabetes, breast cancer and decreased male fertility. They're also related to behavioral issues in children.

- **Propylene glycol** and **polyethylene glycol (PEG):** These are often added to conditioners and cleaning agents. Guess what? They're made from the same chemical that is used to create antifreeze for your car. Barf! There are ties between these compounds and liver, kidney and brain damage. Plus, they're possible carcinogens. They should never go into cosmetics, but they do all the time.

- **Resorcinol:** Commonly added to hair dyes and bleaches, this chemical irritates the skin, is an immunotoxin and causes allergies. The U.S. federal government regulates how much of this chemical employees can be exposed to at work, but manufacturers of beauty and cosmetic products can add it to whatever they please.

- **Siloxanes:** These ingredients are used in cosmetics to give them a smooth, velvety feel. The ingredients are also found in water-repelling windshield coating, building sealants and lubricants, and they are endocrine disruptors and reproductive toxins. Um, yeah, I think I'll pass.

- **Sodium lauryl sulfate** and **sodium laureth sulfate:** These super-common foaming agents are also skin irritants and carcinogens. These nasty culprits commonly cause PMS symptoms (oh, hell no!) and decrease male fertility. They've also been linked to breast cancer. Sometimes "natural" companies will disguise these icky chemicals by saying they're "derived from coconut," but don't buy that BS.

- **Triclosan** and **triclocarban:** Triclosan is often used in liquid soaps; triclocarban, in bar soaps. Both are antimicrobial pesticides that are super-toxic to oceans, lakes and rivers, and all the species that live there. Triclosan also interferes with thyroid function and messes up reproductive hormones. Antibacterial soaps promote bacterial resistance, and — surprise! — you don't need them to fight germs. According to the American Academy of Microbiology, plain old soap and water are just as effective at removing bacteria from the skin and preventing infections.

Check the Label

All this information is kinda scary, I know. But the best way to ensure you're in control and using only the good stuff is to read labels on everything. As you're checking ingredient lists, keep an eye out for the terms *USDA-Certified Organic* or *Ecocert* to make sure you're getting products made with real organic stuff. Do your research and reach out directly to beauty brands if you have any questions or concerns about their products.

Seven Reasons Why DIY Vegan Beauty Is the Best

Sure, you can read labels all day long in the quest to find healthy beauty products. The other solution, of course, is to bypass store-bought altogether; ditch unnatural and potentially hazardous ingredients; and dig in to making your own formulas from skin-loving yummies like organic nut and plant-based butters, waxes, oils, herbs, and fresh fruits and veggies. In case you need a little more convincing, here are my top seven reasons why you'll love making my recipes.

Reason #1: No Bunnies Harmed!

Since you're reading this book, I think it's safe to assume you already have a soft spot for animals. By adopting a cruelty-free beauty routine, you'll reduce the demand for conventional beauty products and, in turn, reduce the number of victims of animal testing. When you make your own vegan beauty products and buy from companies that don't test on animals, you're using your purchasing power for good. And this will increase the demand for more compassionate products.

While many beauty brands are starting to catch up with the times by going cruelty-free (amen and hallelujah!), there are still a bunch of companies that haven't yet made the compassionate switch. You still need to read labels, research companies, and look for vegan and cruelty-free symbols on packaging.

Reason #2: Mama Earth Will Thank You

Homemade beauty products are gentle on you, and they are kinder to our fragile Earth. Mother Nature needs all the help she can get, y'all! The DIY beauty recipes in this book don't contain any of the harmful chemicals that manufacturers use, so this keeps them out of our groundwater, rivers, lakes and oceans. And you can use up any leftover ingredients, like fruits, veggies or tasty cold-pressed nut oils, in salads or smoothies. Even if they've gone bad, you can toss them on the compost heap and give your garden some nutrients it needs.

Since you'll be reusing supplies and containers, DIY beauty products create less garbage that ends up in landfills. No wasteful packaging or nonrecyclable materials are necessary. By making all of your beauty essentials from scratch, you'll be creating something that's good for you and the world, without draining resources and contaminating our big blue marble.

Reason #3: You'll Save Money

It's amazing what you can do with simple staples sitting around in your kitchen. There's absolutely no need to spend $22 on a body scrub, $40 on a facial mask or $6 on a lip balm when you can make these products yourself for pennies on the dollar. Homemade vegan beauty products are extremely easy on the wallet. Everyone I know, me included, is always looking for ways to do more with less.

When you take matters into your own hands and DIY it up, you'll find that the products you make from scratch are indeed more potent and effective than the ones you usually buy. That's because there are no fillers, additives, preservatives or poor-quality ingredients.

Reason #4: Lots of Ingredients Are Already in Your Kitchen

Part of the reason you'll be able to save big bucks is because so many of the ingredients in my DIY recipes are already waiting for you in the pantry and fridge. Here are some examples:

- You buy bananas for breakfast, don't you? Did you know they make a kick-ass moisturizing facial mask that soothes dryness? Just mash and apply!

- Love to cook with coconut oil? You can also use this sweet-smelling oil as a hair mask, shaving cream, moisturizer, makeup remover and lip gloss.

- Have some extra avocado? This always happens after a guac-making sesh. But you don't have to waste it: mash it up and use it as a deep conditioning hair or facial mask.

Keep It Simple
Here's a general rule that applies to beauty products and food alike: if the ingredient list is super-long, that is a big ol' red flag. Whole foods and real natural beauty products are usually made with minimal, simple ingredients.

These are just three ways that you can use fruits, vegetables and other ingredients to make natural beauty products. You'll discover plenty more two-for-one ideas in the recipe section.

Reason #5: You'll Be Healthier with Organics

Since we'll be incorporating food ingredients into our beauty recipes, it's important to focus on organic options. If you're wondering what all the hype about organic food is about, here's a refresher on what it actually means.

The term *organic* refers to the way food is grown and processed. In the United States, products labeled *organic* are regulated under the U.S. Department of Agriculture (USDA) National Organic Program. (Canada and Europe have their own certifying bodies with similar but different regulations.) In the United States, if a product is certified organic, that means that 95% or more of the ingredients in it have been organically produced. That means no harmful hormones or chemicals, such as pesticides, fungicides, herbicides or insecticides.

SPEND YOUR MONEY WHERE IT MATTERS MOST

If you can't afford to buy everything organic (which I *totally* understand), using EWG's handy lists below will help you prioritize your purchases. The Dirty Dozen are the 12 conventionally grown fruits and vegetables most likely to be contaminated with pesticide residues. On the flip side, the Clean Fifteen are the 15 least likely to be contaminated (so you can buy nonorganic if you need to). I keep this info handy whenever I go grocery shopping. The lists are updated annually, so check www.ewg.org every year.

The Dirty Dozen	The Clean Fifteen
Apples	Asparagus
Bell peppers	Avocados
Celery	Cabbage
Cherries	Cantaloupes
Cherry tomatoes	Cauliflower
Cucumbers	Eggplants
Grapes	Grapefruits
Nectarines	Kiwifruits
Peaches	Onions
Spinach	Mangos
Strawberries	Papayas (some seeds are genetically modified; buy organic if you want non-GMO)
Tomatoes	Pineapples
	Sweet corn (some seeds are genetically modified; buy organic if you want non-GMO)
	Sweet peas (frozen)
	Sweet potatoes

Organic farming practices are way better for the environment, too. They respect Mama Earth by encouraging soil and water conservation and reducing pollution. Common organic farming techniques, such as crop rotation, natural pest control and the use of green manure and compost instead of chemical fertilizers, make organic foods a healthier, smarter choice. They are full of the vitamins, minerals, enzymes and micronutrients that Mother Nature intended.

Organic groceries tend to be a bit more expensive. But the long-term payoff is far more valuable. Trust me.

Reason #6: Making Your Own Vegan Beauty Products Is Hella Fun!

I love playing, crafting and experimenting with everything (so say my Pinterest boards). It doesn't matter if it's art, clothes, food, home goods, trinkets or beauty products — I lurve them all. It's such a satisfying, empowering feeling to melt a little of this, mash and mix a little of that, sprinkle something here and there, and then Boom! You have the most luxurious skin-, hair- and body-care formulas you can imagine. And the fun doesn't stop there, because ...

Reason #7: Giving Vegan Beauty Products as Gifts Is Even Nicer

Once you've DIY-ed beauty products for yourself, you'll be excited to make them for your friends and family, too. I don't know about y'all, but nothing beats handmade goodies for me. They are literally the *best* gifts ever.

Not only will you be giving your peeps healthy, cruelty-free alternatives to the products they usually use, but also, your gift will enhance their natural beauty. Best of all, it may inspire them to make their own DIY vegan goodies. You can start your own vegan makeup and beauty-product movement!

Packaging your creations with flowers, twine, branches and berries is a natural and cute way to complement them. It will make your loved ones feel extra warm-'n-fuzzy, too! And to get you started, you'll find my guide to creating labels and packaging for DIY beauty-product gifts on page 261.

Clear Out the Old to Make Room for the New

Now that we've covered all the bases, I encourage you to go through your arsenal of beauty staples in the bathroom. Check them for the toxins you've learned about on pages 28 through 31, and start planning a cruelty-free beauty makeover. There's no rush or pressure to take the plunge overnight, so choose a pace that's budget-friendly and comfortable for you.

Most importantly, have fun experimenting. I really encourage you to play around with the ingredients and let your inner mad scientist run wild when you're making the beauty recipes in this book. Most of them are highly adaptable, so it's almost impossible to take a wrong turn. Just listen to your intuition and common sense.

All right, beauty bunnies, get ready to moisturize with sweet almond oil, scrub your skin and lips with brown sugar and coconut oil, take baths in nondairy nut milks and salts, and glow with naturally spice-filled cosmetics. Info on the essentials you need is coming up next.

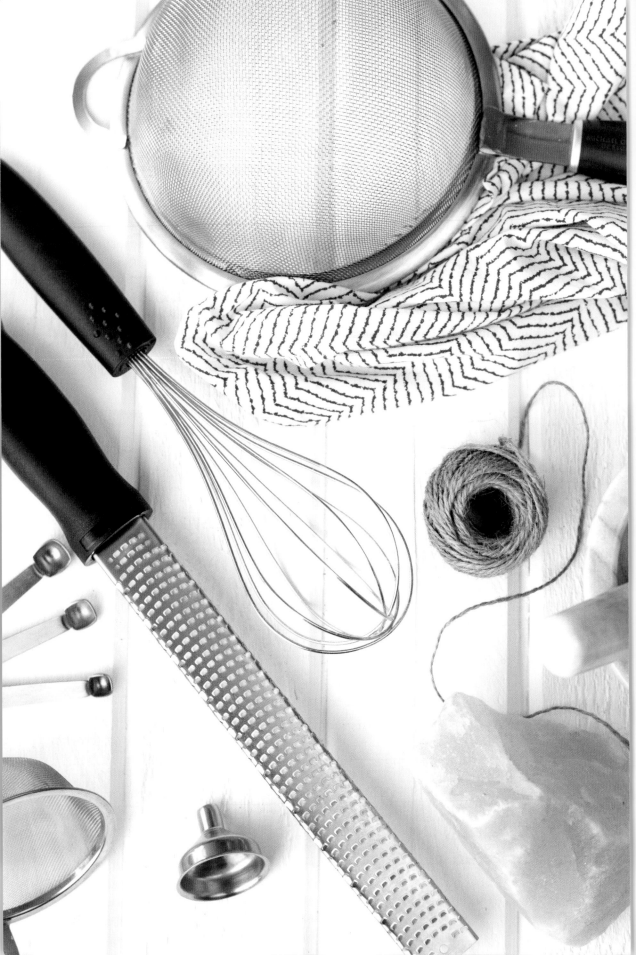

Chapter 3

Essential Vegan Ingredients and Equipment

One of the best parts about making beauty products from scratch is that you probably already have most of the ingredients and tools in your kitchen. While there is a nearly endless list of things you *could* use, in this chapter, I'll highlight the most essential ingredients, tools and equipment that you'll need to make the recipes in this book. If you're looking to keep it über-simple, check out the Keep-It-Simple Staples chart (page 56). It contains enough to get you started, and you can upgrade as you go.

Tools and Supplies

Many of these tools are already in your kitchen, but you'll probably want to invest in a set that you'll use solely for making beauty products. You don't want your pancakes to taste like face cream, right?

- Double boiler, or saucepan and metal or heatproof glass bowl
- Dry measuring cups (for dry and some semi-liquid ingredients); typically, they come in sets of 1 cup, ½ cup, ⅓ cup and ¼ cup
- Liquid measuring cups, each with a spout and measurements marked on the outside of the cup

Buying Guide

Need some shopping advice? You'll find my recommendations on the best places to buy all of these ingredients in the Resources section (page 262).

- Measuring spoons
  (for dry and liquid ingredients)
- Mixing bowls
- Food scale; a digital scale with a tare
  button is really convenient
- Box grater and/or rasp grater
- Mortar and pestle
- Small blender or food processor; these
  recipes produce smallish portions,
  so I like to use a baby-food blender
  because it's the perfect size and affordable
- Spice grinder
- Silicone molds
- Cutting boards
- Containers for finished products: glass bottles with lids, glass jars
  with lids, glass spray bottles, canning jars with lids and tins
- Pipettes or eyedroppers
- Small funnel
- Fine-mesh sieve
- Cheesecloth

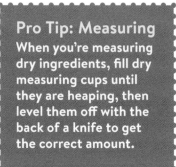

Pro Tip: Measuring
When you're measuring
dry ingredients, fill dry
measuring cups until
they are heaping, then
level them off with the
back of a knife to get
the correct amount.

Carrier Oils

Carrier oils — derived from beans, seeds and nuts — are also called base oils. They are used to dilute essential oils before they're "carried" to the skin. Carrier oils are loaded with vitamins, minerals and essential fatty acids, which can work wonders for your skin. When you're stocking up on them, you'll want to buy cold-pressed and unrefined oils for the most part. There are a few exceptions to this rule; if it's OK to buy refined or partially refined oil, I'll let you know in the info below.

Apricot kernel oil: This is a mild, moisturizing oil that's easily absorbed by the skin. It's best for mature, sensitive and dry-skin peeps. Apricot kernel oil is also versatile: use it in face and body creams, lotions, balms, lip treatments, shampoos, conditioners and soaps.

Argan oil: Light and easy for the skin to absorb, argan oil contains tocopherols (vitamin E), phenols, carotene, squalene (the good, vegetable-derived kind, not the squalene that's made from shark liver oil) and fatty acids. These antioxidants make it a powerful wrinkle fighter and stretch-mark reducer. It works well straight-up out of the bottle, and it's a nice addition to lotions and creams.

Avocado oil: This golden oil is ultra-moisturizing and skin softening, so it's wicked for treating eczema and psoriasis. It's packed with vitamins, amino acids and fatty acids. It also contains natural sun protection factor (SPF), so it can protect your skin from the sun's damaging rays. Avocado oil works well on all skin types, but it's especially kind to sensitive, dry and mature skin.

Castor oil (refined OK): Pressed from castor beans, this oil acts as a barrier agent on the skin: it seals in moisture and is an ideal ingredient in protective, soothing creams and lotions. It is great for all skin types, but acne-prone and sensitive types love it best of all.

Coconut oil (refined OK): This oil is everywhere for good reason! Protective, antioxidant-rich, antimicrobial, moisturizing and blessed with natural SPF, coconut oil is great for most skin types, but because it has a comedogenic rating of 4 (see chart, page 47) and may cause breakouts, it's not recommended for oily skin. Coconut oil has a sweet, yummy scent, and can be used in a million and one ways. I especially like to add it to lip balms, lotions, creams and hair products. Check out the in-depth profile (page 42) for more info on this amazing oil.

Grapeseed oil (partially refined OK): This is a terrific base oil for creams, lotions and serums because it's easily absorbed. It's nice and gentle for people with skin sensitivities because it is naturally hypoallergenic. You can use grapeseed oil on all kinds of skin; it's particularly good for dry and sensitive folks.

THE COOLEST: COCONUT OIL

Coconut oil is one of Mama Nature's greatest gifts. Why? It's affordable and easy to find, smells delicious, tastes über-yummy (especially on pancakes and cinnamon toast) and is good for you. What more could you ask for?

Coconut oil is extremely versatile. It makes my skin and hair feel silky smooth. Babies love it: you can use it as a gentle moisturizer and a soothing baby booty cream. Whether you eat coconut oil or use it to beautify yourself, you'll be stoked with all the uses you'll find for it. Check out some of my faves in the box below.

15 Wonderful Uses for Coconut Oil

- Cooking oil (substitute for butter or veggie oils in recipes)
- Skin moisturizer
- Deodorant (see page 232)
- Toothpaste (see page 236)
- Body scrub (see page 145)
- Body balm (just whip it with some melted shea or cocoa butter)
- Hair mask or deep conditioner
- Makeup remover
- Massage oil
- Hair de-frizzer
- Diaper cream
- Stretch-mark reducer
- Personal lubricant
- Cuticle softener
- Natural bug repellent (just mix with essential oil made from catnip, rosemary or mint)

A Closer Look at Coconut Oil in Action

- **Skin care.** Whether you have cracked heels or crusty elbows, a little bit of coconut oil goes a long way in the healing department (it also has antibacterial and antifungal properties). If you're brave and don't have reservations about smearing oil on your face, the teensiest amount of coconut oil can help fight wrinkles. It also does an amazing job at removing makeup. Coconut oil has made its way into a whole bunch of fancy-schmancy skin-care lines, but why pay a bundle to someone else when you can DIY?

- **Hair care.** I first discovered I could use coconut oil as a leave-in conditioner at a photo shoot. The makeup artist who was doing my hair suggested I rock some to tame my frizzies. She then whipped out a jar, dipped her finger in it, rubbed the oil between her palms and applied it to my damaged, split-endy hair. I have to admit, my mane looked much healthier and *fine*, and I learned a new beauty trick to boot. You can also apply coconut oil to your scalp to prevent dandruff.

- **Lip care.** Dab a bit of straight-up coconut oil on your lips next time they're feeling thirsty for some moisture. This is the perfect solution when you run out of your favorite vegan lip balm.

- **Don't forget cooking!** Coconut oil is one of the healthiest oils you can use. Studies cite its ability to do everything from lower your blood pressure to increase your metabolism. Coconut oil is also the bomb for cooking because it has a sort of nutty, sweet flavor that complements a slew of desserts and savory foods.

More Coconut Love

I think it's obvs, but I'd like to declare my love of all things coconut to the world. And it's not just coconut oil I adore. I lurve fresh young coconut water, juicy coconut pulp, coconut milk (especially in smoothies and on cereal), Mahalo Candy Bars (think gluten-free, vegan Almond Joys) — anything with lots o' coconut! That means there are lots of coconut-scented lotions, body sprays and perfume oils in my collection. Turn to the recipe section, starting on page 59, for more ways to add my fave fruit to your DIY beauty products.

Hemp seed oil: Don't freak, y'all, this is not weed oil — there's no detectable tetrahydrocannabinol (THC) in here that will get you stoned. Hemp seed oil is a super-rich, nutrient-dense oil, loaded with vitamins, essential omega-3 and omega-6 fatty acids, proteins and lots more. It has a nutty aroma and pretty deep-green color. The skin soaks it up well, so it's a good moisturizer. Hemp seed oil is also anti-inflammatory and helps stimulate cell growth. I use it in creams, lotions, facial or body oils, shaving products, lip balms and hair treatments. It works on all skin types, especially dry and mature. This is an oil you'll want to keep in the fridge.

Jojoba oil: It's referred to as oil, but psych! Jojoba oil is actually a liquid wax ester that acts a lot like human skin oil (aka sebum). Naturally antibiotic, antiviral, antifungal, analgesic, anti-inflammatory and hypoallergenic, jojoba oil also contains vitamin E, and omega-6 and omega-9 essential fatty acids. It's effective for all skin types. Bonus: it has a longer shelf life than most oils (up to 3 years). Check out the opposite page for more on this supercharged oil.

Olive oil: Talk about an all-around winner. Olive oil can be used for everything from cosmetics to serums to body oils to hair-care treatments — and I'm not even mentioning how good it is in cooking! Even better, olive oil is budget-friendly, so you can use lots of it. It has excellent moisturizing properties in all sorts of beauty recipes. Olive oil works well for most skin types; avoid it if you have oily or acne-prone skin.

Rose hip seed oil: This beauty is considered a dry oil, which means it's easily absorbed and won't leave a greasy residue on your skin. It's extremely high in essential fatty acids and works wonders on scars, wrinkles and fine lines. It's a mega-hydrator that penetrates the skin immediately, so I love to add it to creams, lotions, facial oils and serums. This is an oil you should keep in the fridge.

Sunflower oil (refined OK): Not just a pretty face, the sunflower gives us this easily absorbable oil that's chock-full of unsaturated fatty acids, including oleic acid. It offers the skin plenty of vitamin E, so it is extremely nourishing. It's a great conditioner and is especially talented at pampering dry, weathered and mature skin.

Sweet almond oil (refined or partially refined OK): This heavenly oil contains essential fatty acids, plus lots of vitamins A and E. It is similar to the natural sebum our bodies produce, so it penetrates the skin easily and does an amazing job at softening and conditioning skin and hair. It also helps relieve itching, soreness, dryness and inflammation. That makes it great for all skin types, but especially beneficial for people with eczema.

> **Pro Tip: Storing Carrier Oils**
> You can keep most carrier oils in a cool, dark place for up to two years. (Jojoba will last for up to three years!) Some may require refrigeration to keep them fresh; follow the instructions on the bottle or in the descriptions on pages 41 and 44.

THE JOYS OF JOJOBA OIL

Jo jo jo! It's time to talk about another of my favorite versatile beauty oils. Jojoba oil is the answer to all of your beauty prayers — trust me. It's affordable, easy to use, and readily available, and will transform your skin, hair and nails for the better. Check out all of these fab ways to use it:

- **Body oil.** Use jojoba as a massage oil (I like to add a few drops of lavender essential oil to it first). It also makes a great all-over body moisturizer after a nice, relaxing bath or shower. It absorbs quickly and leaves your skin feeling like silk.

- **Body scrub.** Jojoba is the key to a perfect scrub. Seriously. Mix granulated sugar with jojoba oil and add a few drops of your favorite essential oil(s), mix and enjoy. You're welcome!

- **Facial moisturizer.** Jojoba oil helps balance skin's natural sebum levels: it moisturizes dry skin and chills out grease production in oily skin. You can rest assured that using jojoba oil on your face will not cause zits. Apply a few drops directly to your skin, or mix it with your favorite moisturizer for some extra-hydrating oomph.

- **Leave-in hair treatment.** If you have dry or damaged hair (like I do), rub a few drops of jojoba oil between your palms and work it through your hair. Make sure you really hit up the extra-dry, frizzy, strawlike bits. Your mane will love you (and vice versa).

- **Lip conditioner.** I like adding a dab of jojoba oil to my lips after a much-needed sugary lip scrub treatment. It makes my smacker extra smoochable.

- **Makeup remover.** Soak a cotton ball in jojoba oil and gently rub it all over your face to get rid of foundation, powder, mascara and everything else. It's the best makeup remover ever, and it leaves your skin perfectly conditioned.

- **Nail conditioner.** Slathering jojoba oil on your nails and cuticles on a semiregular basis will smooth out all those cracked, ridgy areas so your hands look their best.

How to Infuse Carrier Oils

Some of the recipes in this book ask you to infuse carrier oils with herbs, flowers, spices, coffee or tea. These infusions add extra beneficial properties to your skin-care formulations. There are two ways to do this: the quick zap-it-with-heat way (holla!) or the slow let-it-chill-with-Mother-Nature's-help way.

- **Quick Heat Infusion.** Combine the carrier oil(s) and dry ingredient(s) in a slow cooker. The slow cooker should be small enough that the oil(s) completely covers the dry ingredient(s). Cover and cook on Low for 8 to 10 hours, stirring every hour. Let cool completely.

- **Slow Cold Infusion.** Combine the carrier oil(s) and dry ingredient(s) in a glass jar with a tight-fitting lid. The jar should be small enough that the oil(s) completely covers the dry ingredient(s). Seal the jar and let it stand for 2 to 6 weeks in a warm place, shaking once a day. The longer it stands, the stronger the infusion — the timing is your call. If the jar is dark blue or amber, you can place it in direct sunlight, if you like.

Once your mixture is done steeping, strain it through a fine-mesh sieve lined with cheesecloth. Make sure to squeeze out every last drop of oil! Now it's ready to add to your DIY facial oils, creams, serums, lotions or pretty much anything else your heart desires.

Meet Your Beauty Oil BFFs

Since I love and rely on beauty oils to help keep my skin looking young and fresh, I thought I'd quickly go over which oils are the best for your skin. Oils that can clog your pores are referred to as *comedogenic*. Ones that won't are referred to as *noncomedogenic*. To recap, comedogenic = acne and blackheads (bad); noncomedogenic = clear skin (super-awesome). The latter are the ones you wanna slather all over your face and body.

Believe it or not, lots of oils have antiseptic and sebum-balancing characteristics that actually fight acne, such as jojoba, rose hip seed and castor oils. I know, I know — it sounds counterintuitive to slather oil on your face to fight zits. But noncomedogenic oils are the *best* moisturizers and wrinkle fighters. They contain zero filler ingredients and are brimming with skin-loving power players, including antioxidants, vitamins and essential fatty acids. So what's good and what's not-so-good? Check out the chart on the opposite page.

COMEDOGENIC RATINGS OF OILS AND PLANT BUTTERS

The pore-clogging powers of oils are rated on a scale of 0–5, with 0 being the least likely to be comedogenic and 5 being the most likely.

Rating	Oil	Uses
0 Noncomedogenic (Won't Clog Pores)	Argan oil Hemp seed oil Safflower oil Shea butter Sunflower oil	Ideal for face and body
1 Low Comedogenic Properties	Calendula oil Castor oil Pomegranate oil Rose hip seed oil Sea buckthorn oil	OK to use on face and body
2 Moderately Low Comedogenic Properties	Apricot kernel oil Avocado oil Baobab seed oil Borage oil Evening primrose oil Grapeseed oil Hazelnut oil Jojoba oil Olive oil Pumpkin seed oil Sesame oil Sweet almond oil Tamanu oil Vitamin A palmitate oil Vitamin E oil	OK to use on face and body
3 Moderate Comedogenic Properties	Corn oil Cotton seed oil Soybean oil	OK to use on face and body in moderation
4 Fairly High Comedogenic Properties	Cocoa butter Coconut oil	OK to use on body in moderation; avoid if you have acne-prone skin
5 High Comedogenic Properties	Wheat germ oil	OK to use on body in moderation; avoid if you have acne-prone skin

Plant Butters

Made from seeds, roots and other plant sources, natural butters are fabulous for making your skin insanely silky and soft. You can use them straight-up, or you can melt and whip them to add to lotions, creams, scrubs, balms and more. The most natural options are made by expeller-pressing the seeds or other plant parts, without adding solvents to extract the butter. It's OK to use a refined version of a butter, but raw or unrefined versions are best.

Cocoa butter: This moisture-rich solid butter is made by pressing the roasted seeds of the cacao tree. It gives lotions and creams a rich, creamy consistency. And hey, it smells so yummy, like chocolate!

Kokum butter: Snowy white kokum butter is pressed from the seeds of the *Garcinia* tree, which is also known by the Indian name *kokum*. The butter is known for its emollient and regenerative properties. It's a terrific ingredient to add to body lotions, butters and creams.

Mango butter: Mango butter has skin-nourishing properties that are similar to those of shea and cocoa butters. It's loaded with essential fatty acids and is emollient, so it helps soften, moisturize and protect your skin.

Shea butter: This is a classic ingredient you'll find in so many natural beauty products. Shea butter is a wonderful emollient and is rich in vitamins A and E, so it makes an amazing hydrating component in lotions and body butters.

Vegetable Waxes

Since compassion is the name of the game, we're gonna ditch the beeswax found in most commercial beauty products. Fly free, little bees! We'll replace it with plant-based, bee-friendly, vegan waxes to help thicken recipes and solidify salves, lip balms, lipsticks, lotion bars and solid perfumes. Natural veggie waxes lock in moisture, protect the skin and make application so, so smooth.

Candelilla wax: This wax is derived from the leaves of the small candelilla shrub that's native to Mexico and the southwestern United States. It's probably the most popular plant-based wax for DIY beauty recipes, and is fabulous for making creams, body butters, salves, ointments, balms, pomades and lipsticks.

Carnauba wax: Made from the leaves of a Brazilian palm tree known as the "tree of life," carnauba wax is one of the hardest natural plant-based waxes available. It works well in recipes for lip balms, salves, creams and lotions.

Soy wax: Moisture-rich and loaded with vitamin E, soy wax is ideal for making treatments for psoriasis, eczema, dry skin, cracked skin, cracked heels and rough cuticles.

Clays

Clay, a dense, mineral-rich type of soil, has been used for centuries for its amazing ability to cleanse, tone and detoxify the body. It works because the particles it contains generally have a negative electromagnetic charge, while most toxins under your skin have a positive charge. This allows clay to draw out impurities easily.

Bentonite clay: Bentonite comes from volcanic ash that occurs naturally in the United States. It's loaded with silica, aluminum, iron and magnesium. It's a powerful healing clay with antibacterial and oil-absorbing properties that help de-gunk pores and clear acne. It's commonly used in recipes for homemade facial masks, dry shampoos and deodorants.

French green clay: Also known as illite clay or sea clay, this clay gets its green color from a combination of iron oxides and decomposed plant matter. It's made up of tiny molecules that sop up oils and toxins from your skin.

Fuller's earth clay: If you have acne-prone skin, definitely stock up on this clay, because it has drying and oil-absorbing powers. It also has a mild bleaching effect on the skin, which can help with hyperpigmentation. Always make sure to buy the cosmetic-grade variety of this clay.

> ### Did You Know?
> Since the late 1940s, fuller's earth clay has been used in commercial non-clumping cat litter, because it has superb absorption powers. Kitty litter facial mask, anyone?

Rhassoul clay: This reddish-brown clay from Morocco is also known as red clay, red Moroccan clay, ghassoul clay and oxide clay. Rhassoul clay can be used in detoxifying cleansers, skin conditioners, shampoos and facial masks. It improves skin tone and texture without leaving your skin dry or flaky.

White kaolin clay: Also known as white cosmetic clay, kaolin is mild and perfect for people with dry or sensitive skin. Unlike the other clays above, this one won't draw out oil from the skin. White kaolin clay is a terrific ingredient to use in soaps, facial masks and bath fizzies. It acts as a mild exfoliant when used to make a cleanser or scrub.

Sugars and Salts

Sugars and salts are amazing exfoliants. Sugar is also rich in natural enzymes. Both are lovely multipurpose ingredients: after you're done sloughing off dead skin cells with your very own personalized facial scrub, you can celebrate by baking a big ol' vegan cake!

Dead Sea salt: This one contains a large percentage of magnesium, sulfates and potassium. It's great for bath salts and body scrubs.

Epsom salt: Surprise! While it looks a lot like salt, this isn't actually salt — it's pure magnesium sulfate in crystal form. Epsom salt is terrific in bath salts to help soothe and relax sore muscles.

Himalayan pink salt: These pretty pink crystals are one of the purest salts available for culinary and beauty uses. They are especially wonderful in bath salts and scrubs.

Sea salt: Similar to table salt but without the added iodine, natural sea salt is an antibacterial exfoliant that's loaded with minerals. Fine grinds work best for body scrubs and bath bombs.

Vegan sugars: Bone char — a porous, black, granular material produced by charring animal bones (say whaaat!?) — is used to process many types of commercial sugar, including brown sugar and confectioner's sugar. Yuck! Thank goodness, health food stores often have specially labeled vegan sugars that skip this nasty step. Beet sugar is usually a vegan-friendly option, too.

Pro Tip:
Go Fine or Go Home

Additional Exfoliants

Exfoliants are super-effective at removing dead skin cells and revealing younger, healthier looking skin. There are a couple of simple ones I use in all sorts of DIY vegan beauty recipes:

Almond meal: This is made by grinding unblanched almonds with their skins still on until they're granular (but not pasty — that's almond butter). Almond meal exfoliates, smooths and softens the skin; reduces inflammation; and absorbs excess oil.

Rolled oats: Not just a breakfast hero, oats are anti-inflammatory, gentle and soothing to the skin. They exfoliate without causing irritation.

Essential Oils

Plants produce essential oils for a variety of reasons: to attract pollinators (like bees), to protect against bacteria or fungi, to scare away pests and to keep other plants from growing too close. These oils can be removed from the plants through the process of distillation for us humans to use for medicinal or cosmetic purposes.

Essential oils can be extracted from almost any plant component. They can be made from leaves (such as eucalyptus), grasses (such as lemongrass), seeds (such as fennel), fruit zest (such as mandarin orange), flowers (such as rose), wood or bark (such as cedarwood), roots and rhizomes (such as ginger), resins (such as frankincense) and herb flowers or parts (such as rosemary).

Using essential oils can bring a basic beauty recipe to life, adding lovely aromas and colors. Essential oils are, well, *essential* when it comes to customizing your skin-care products so they suit your skin to a T. You'll discover this as you explore the recipes in Part Two of this book. Here are some of the most popular essential oils and their unique and beneficial properties:

Chamomile: anti-inflammatory, calming, soothing

Clove: antibacterial, antiparasitic, antioxidant

Eucalyptus: invigorating, antiseptic, antibiotic, antifungal

Evening primrose: antibacterial, anti-inflammatory, antiaging

Frankincense: anti-inflammatory, antiaging, age spot–reducing

Grapefruit: cellulite-fighting

Jasmine: anti-inflammatory, antiseptic, aphrodisiac

Lavender: healing, calming

Lemon: antiseptic, antibacterial, antifungal

Myrrh: antiseptic, infection-reducing, stretch mark–reducing

Oregano: antimicrobial

Peppermint: anti-inflammatory, antibacterial, antifungal, antiseptic, cooling, soothing, dandruff- and acne-fighting

Rose: antibacterial, anti-inflammatory, antiseptic, hydrating, antiaging, acne-fighting, moisturizing

Rose hip seed: antiaging, anti-inflammatory, moisturizing

Rosemary: healthy hair–promoting

Sweet orange: astringent, antifungal, acne-fighting

Tea tree: antibacterial, antiviral, antifungal, odor-reducing, immunity-stimulating, dandruff- and acne-fighting

Ylang-ylang: antiseptic, aphrodisiac, mildly antidepressant

Essential Oils for Every Budget

It's true, some essential oils cost a pretty penny. The good news is that there are lots of recipes that call for affordable essential oils. Start with those, and then purchase some more-expensive options as your finances allow. Another point in favor of spending a little cheddar for the good stuff? Essential oils last: you can invest in pricier ones, knowing you'll be able to use them in tons of recipes.

Whether they're budget-friendly or turbo-spendy, essential oils are worth the cash. They're brimming with aromatherapeutic compounds and offer a slew of benefits for your beauty, health and well-being. For example, lavender essential oil (one of the more affordable essential oils) makes a lovely addition to facial masks and body washes. It's antiseptic, antifungal and anti-inflammatory, so it helps fight acne and reduce scarring. Lavender essential oil also soothes anxiety and reduces stress. So it's win-win!

PRICE POINTS OF ESSENTIAL OILS

Affordable	Pricier	Break the Bank
• Clove	• Bergamot	• Blue chamomile
• Eucalyptus	• Cinnamon	• Carrot seed
• Grapefruit	• Frankincense	• Jasmine
• Lavender	• Juniper berry	• Myrrh
• Lemon	• Patchouli	• Rose
• Lemongrass	• Sage	• Sandalwood
• Peppermint	• Thyme	• Vanilla absolute
• Rosemary	• Ylang-ylang	
• Spearmint		
• Sweet orange		
• Tangerine		
• Tea tree		

ESSENTIAL OILS DURING PREGNANCY

So you're baby bumping? Congrats! It's important to know which essential oils are OK and which are verboten for baby's safety. The oils on the left below are generally considered safe to use during pregnancy, even when you're in your second and third trimesters. The ones on the right below should be avoided throughout your pregnancy. In any case, check with your physician before you start using any essential oil.

Generally Considered Safe	Avoid
• Black pepper	• Basil
• Cypress	• Bergamot
• Eucalyptus	• Carrot seed
• Frankincense	• Cedarwood
• Geranium	• Cinnamon
• German and Roman chamomile	• Citronella
• Ginger	• Clary sage
• Grapefruit	• Clove
• Lavender	• Fennel
• Lemon	• Jasmine
• Lemongrass	• Juniper berry
• Neroli	• Lemon eucalyptus
• Palmarosa	• Myrrh
• Patchouli	• Nutmeg
• Peppermint	• Rose
• Rosewood	• Rosemary
• Sandalwood	• Sage
• Spearmint	• Wintergreen
• Sweet orange	
• Tangerine	
• Tea tree	
• Ylang-ylang	

Never take essential oils internally without talking to your doctor. Many are not safe for ingestion, so it pays to check first.

Cautions: Bergamot Essential Oil

While bergamot essential oil offers a number of positive effects on the body, there are a couple of things you have to be mindful of when using this oil. First, it is phototoxic, meaning it can increase your skin's vulnerability to sun damage (especially if you have sensitive skin). It's especially important not to use it if you are also taking photosensitizing drugs, such as ciprofloxacin (Cipro), doxycycline, levofloxacin (Levaquin), lomefloxacin (Maxaquin), norfloxacin (Noroxin), ofloxacin (Floxin), sulfamethoxazole (Septra) and tetracycline. Taking these drugs and using bergamot essential oil simultaneously can cause serious adverse reactions.

Also, it's best to avoid taking bergamot essential oil orally if you have a potassium deficiency. It can decrease your stores of this mineral further, causing muscle cramps and twitching. Pregnant and nursing women, and young children, should never use bergamot essential oil either internally or externally on the skin. Your best bet? Always consult your physician before adding any new essential oil to your arsenal.

Always keep anything made with bergamot essential oil away from light. Store the oil and potions made with it in a dark glass bottle in a cool, dark place. When exposed to sunlight, a component in it, called bergapten, becomes toxic.

KEEP-IT-SIMPLE STAPLES

If you're new to making your own beauty products, the lists of potential ingredients might seem overwhelming at first, so start by setting yourself up with the basics. The simple ingredients below will create the largest number of recipes with the smallest investment. As you become familiar with the DIY process — and start to enjoy it — you can add more ingredients and equipment. The sky's the limit when it comes to homemade vegan beauty.

Ingredient	Use It In
Aromatherapy essential oils	Almost anything; try my versatile favorites (lavender, peppermint, sweet orange and lemon), and don't forget tea tree oil, because it's antifungal, antiseptic, antimicrobial and antibacterial (plus, it fights acne)
Arrowroot powder or cornstarch	Deodorants, dry shampoos, body powders, makeup
Baking soda	Gentle facial scrubs, shampoos, deodorants, toothpastes, bath bombs
Candelilla wax	Body moisturizers, facial creams, salves, lip balms, lipsticks, solid perfumes
Cider vinegar	Facial toners, cleansers, hair treatments
Cocoa butter	Body moisturizers, facial creams, deodorants, creams, salves, lipsticks, solid perfumes
Coconut oil	Body moisturizers, exfoliating treatments, scrubs, hair treatments, shaving creams, toothpastes
Dried herbs and flowers	Bath bombs, facial steams, oil infusions
Green tea	Soothing treatments; naturally full of antioxidants, it's also anti-inflammatory, astringent and antibacterial, and helps reduce puffiness and large pores
Liquid carrier oils, such as olive, sweet almond, grapeseed and jojoba	Body moisturizers, massage oils, scrubs, facial creams, salves, essential oil perfumes
Salts	Scrubs, hairsprays
Shea butter	Body moisturizers, facial creams, deodorants, salves, lipsticks, solid perfumes
Sugars	Scrubs, hairsprays
Unscented liquid castile soap	Cleansers for hands, face, body, makeup brushes
Vitamin E oil	Skin-healing treatments; it reduces the appearance of scars and promotes healing, and is a natural preservative
Witch hazel	Tons of treatments; it's astringent and mildly antibacterial, and it shrinks pores and fights acne

Buying Gluten-Free Ingredients

The recipes in this book are gluten-free. Lots of people are following a gluten-free lifestyle for many different reasons, from celiac disease to suspected gluten intolerance to personal choice. This means not eating or using any products that contain gluten, a natural protein found in some grains, such as wheat, barley and rye.

To ensure that your DIY beauty products are gluten-free, make sure you read every label on every ingredient you use. If it says that the ingredient has been packaged in a gluten-free facility or that it's gluten-free, you're generally good to go. If not, look for an alternative brand that does offer that guarantee.

But remember that although some ingredients are naturally gluten-free, they may be cross-contaminated when they're packaged. A good example of this is oats, which may contain residues from gluten-containing grains that are processed in the same facility. In this case, look for labels that promise "pure, uncontaminated oats."

Keep It Fresh

Since the recipes in this book are completely natural and devoid of any chemical preservatives, it's important to note that they have a shorter shelf life than conventional, store-bought beauty products. The shelf life is noted for each recipe in this book unless it's a one-time-use formula.

To maintain optimal freshness, store your homemade beauty products in dark containers and/or dark cabinets to keep them away from light. Make sure your storage area is cool and dry, too, because bacteria thrive in moist, warm environments. Storing your homemade beauty products in the fridge can extend their shelf life, as well.

All-Natural Preservatives

When you're concocting your recipes, you can add a few drops of the following all-natural preservatives to extend their shelf life:

- Coconut oil
- Grapefruit seed extract
- Rosemary oil extract
- Vitamin E oil

Part Two
The Recipes

Chapter 4

Face Care

No-Brainer Makeup Remover... 64

Moisturizing Makeup Remover... 65

Pucker-Up Peppermint
Lip Scrub... 66

Forever Young Antiaging
Cleanser... 68

Gentle Rose Water Cleanser... 69

Simple Castile Soap Cleansers
(for Acne-Prone, Mature
or Dry Skin)... 70

Basic Oil Cleansers
(for Normal, Dry, Mature
or Acne-Prone Skin)... 72

Acne-Away Cleanser... 73

Basic Toner for All Skin Types... 75

Pore-Shrinking Basil Toner... 76

Toner for Acne-Prone Skin... 78

Rose Water Toner for Dry
or Sensitive Skin... 80

Lovely Lavender
Fresh-Face Spray... 82

Gentle Antiaging Toner... 83

Zit-Zapping Blemish Stick... 84

Potent Antiaging Rose Serum... 87

Customizable Hemp Seed
Facial Oil... 88

Kick-Ass Wake-Up
Coffee Serum... 90

Miracle Antiaging
Night Cream... 91

Creamy Dreamy
Rooibos Moisturizer... 92

Basic Facial Scrub... 94

Not-So-Basic Facial Scrub... 95

Pore De-Gunking Coffee
Facial Scrub... 96

Hella-Bomb Oatmeal
Facial Scrub... 99

Fruity AHA Facial Peel... 100

Matcha Green Goddess
Facial Mask... 103

Black Forest Chocolate Cake
Facial Mask... 104

Green Clay Detox
Facial Mask... 106

Skin-Quenching Facial Mask... 107

Mellow (Yellow) Out Your Skin
Turmeric Facial Mask... 108

Zit-Blasting Bananarama
Facial Mask... 110

Party Like It's 1999
Antiaging Facial Mask... 111

Avocado Banana Skin-Soothing
Smoothie Facial Mask... 112

Antioxidant Blueberry Delight
Smoothie Facial Mask... 115

Just-Glow-with-It Spinach
Smoothie Facial Mask... 116

Sunny's Homemade
Sunscreen... 118

FACE-CARE BASICS

Let's talk skin care. Like I said earlier, what you put *on* your body is just as important as what you put *in* your body. You may already know that excessive sun exposure, air pollution, poor diet, smoking and stress can prematurely age you. But are you wise to what's in all those conventional "miracle creams" that claim to turn back the hands of time (and cost a pretty penny)? They often contain super-sketchy, toxic ingredients, including artificial preservatives, artificial dyes, carcinogens, hormone disruptors, skin irritants and so on. Pretty shouldn't have to look this ugly, am I right?

If you're freaked out, good! But learning this means change is just around the corner. In this section, we're going to gently clean, tenderly tone, ditch dead skin cells, maximize moisture, zap zits and more using pure, natural ingredients. Scrumptious homemade cleansers, toners, facial masks, peels and scrubs, here we come!

Apply Your Skin-Care Potions in the Correct Order

Peeps, I am militant about following this skin-care regimen. Seriously — *you must do these things in this order!* I swear, you're going be stoked with the long-term results. If you've ever wondered whether you're supposed to apply moisturizer before or after eye cream or looked at a serum and thought "WTF?", I'm here to help.

Step 1. Makeup remover. De-gunk your face and get rid of dirt, oil and makeup before you start the cleansing process.

Step 2. Cleanser. Use a cleanser that suits your skin type: dry, sensitive, oily, acne-prone, mature or combo. Try to use products that don't contain artificial fragrances, parabens (and other potentially toxic preservatives) or harsh detergents, which can dry your skin out. That's counterproductive.

Step 3. Toner. Toners help restore your skin to its natural pH. They are often mega-hydrating and packed with active ingredients that treat and soothe skin. They also help shrink the appearance of pores.

Step 4. Zit cream or spot treatment. If your skin needs this, use it after cleansing and toning.

Step 5. Serum. Quick-absorbing, nutrient-rich serums usually come in gel or oil form and cater to specific skin types.

Step 6. Eye cream and/or antiaging serum. Eye creams are formulated to protect and nourish the delicate skin around your eyes. Antiaging serums are essential for combating the appearance of fine lines and wrinkles.

Step 7. Moisturizer and/or antiaging oil. Light moisturizers are great for daytime. Save thick, mega-rich and creamy moisturizers and beauty-oil blends for pre-bedtime application.

Optional Steps

- **Exfoliator or scrub.** A couple of times a week, exfoliate your skin using a good facial scrub. Be sure to follow up with toner, serum and moisturizer.

- **Facial mask.** If you're dealing with a bout of stubborn acne or if your skin is begging to be drenched in mega-moisture, treat yourself to a weekly mask. It'll do wonders for your skin, and it's a nice, spa-like way to relax. Be sure to follow up with toner, serum and moisturizer.

No-Brainer Makeup Remover

Commercial makeup remover is something you should stop buying ASAP. No way should you be rubbing all those unnatural ingredients — isododecane, cyclopentasiloxane, caprylic/capric triglyceride, cyclohexasiloxane, phenoxyethanol ... aaaaaagh! — around your delicate eyeballs. This easy-peasy recipe doubles as a light moisturizer, and it does a hella-better job at removing makeup (even waterproof mascara!) than store-bought formulas.

Best for:

♥ All skin types

TOP TIP: It's easy to grow your own aloe vera plant. It's a succulent, which makes it virtually impossible to kill (my kind of plant). I have one of these babies potted in my kitchen, and I've named him Mark RuffAloe, after one of my favorite actors.

★ **Superstar ingredient:** Jojoba is pretty much my go-to carrier oil. It's naturally antibiotic, antiviral, antifungal, analgesic, anti-inflammatory and hypoallergenic. It also contains B complex vitamins, skin-healing vitamin E and a variety of minerals. It's great for face, body, hair and nails.

• Glass jar with lid

1 cup	aloe vera gel (see Top tips, page 82)	250 mL
½ cup	jojoba oil	125 mL

1. In a medium bowl, stir aloe vera gel with jojoba oil until well combined. Spoon into jar.

2. Using a cotton ball or round, gently wipe mixture over facial skin and eye area, repeating as necessary until all makeup is removed.

3. Store at room temperature out of direct sunlight for up to 6 months.

DID YOU KNOW? Aloe vera can also be used to soothe sunburn, alleviate rashes, moisturize dry areas, treat dandruff, brighten skin, fight wrinkles and prevent acne.

Moisturizing Makeup Remover

I used to be on a seemingly endless quest to find the perfect makeup remover. Honestly, it took me years to find my go-to solution. This is hands-down the easiest and best makeup remover ever. It'll have even your stubborn waterproof liner, mascara and matte liquid lipsticks saying, "OK, gotta go. Peace out!"

Best for:

♥ All skin types, especially ▲ Dry

TOP TiP: Five years ago, you'd never have caught me putting straight-up oil on my face to remove makeup. My, how times have changed. But if you're still not keen on it, try adding 1 tsp (5 mL) of pure, unscented, no-tears castile soap to this recipe.

★ **Superstar ingredients:** Jojoba oil is very similar to the sebum produced by your skin, making it an ideal moisturizer. It's non-greasy, absorbs easily and creates a shield against moisture loss.

Both clary sage and frankincense essential oils are eye-safe. Clary sage regulates oil production and reduces inflammation; frankincense is astringent and reduces the appearance of wrinkles.

- Glass jar with lid

¼ cup	jojoba oil	60 mL
5	drops clary sage essential oil (see Caution, below)	5
5	drops frankincense essential oil	5

1. In a small bowl, stir together jojoba oil, clary sage essential oil and frankincense essential oil until well combined. Spoon into jar.

2. Using a cotton ball or round, gently wipe mixture over facial skin and eye area, repeating as necessary until all makeup is removed.

3. Store at room temperature out of direct sunlight for up to 6 months.

DID YOU KNOW?

Jojoba oil won't clog your pores or make you break out, so it's an ideal natural oil for all skin types. It's versatile, too: feel free to use this recipe as a hair mask or a body oil.

Caution: Don't use sage or clary sage in any form if you are pregnant or nursing, or have epilepsy.

Pucker-Up Peppermint Lip Scrub

There's nothing like dry, chapped lips to make smooth lipstick application impossible. Argh! Plus, who wants to make out with a crusty-mouthed beast? Skip the store-bought lip scrub, save yourself some dough and experience the satisfaction of DIY-ing this beauty at home. Peppermint essential oil gives it the ooh-la-la tinglies.

Best for:

♥ All skin types

TOP TIP: If you like your lip scrub to glide more easily, add more jojoba oil, a few drops at a time, until you get the consistency you like.

★ Superstar ingredient: The brown sugar in this recipe will help remove dry, flaky dead skin on your lips, making them kissably soft. Pucker up!

• *Small glass jar with lid*

1 tbsp	packed vegan brown sugar (see Top tip, page 145)	15 mL
1 tsp	jojoba oil (see info, page 65)	5 mL
1/4 tsp	vanilla extract	1 mL
3	drops peppermint essential oil (see Did you know?, page 123)	3

1. In a small bowl, stir together brown sugar, jojoba oil, vanilla extract and peppermint essential oil until sugar is moistened. Spoon into jar.

2. Using index finger or toothbrush, apply scrub to lips. Gently scrub, in circles, for 10 seconds.

3. Rinse lips with warm water and pat dry with a towel. Follow with Luscious Lip Balm (page 219) or another favorite vegan lip balm.

4. Store at room temperature out of direct sunlight for up to 6 months.

DID YOU KNOW? Lip scrubs are typically designed to be sweet and yummy, just in case you accidentally ingest some.

Forever Young Antiaging Cleanser

Looking for your own fountain of youth? This cleanser wipes away the years in the gentlest possible way.

Best for:

♥ All skin types, especially ■ Mature and ▲ Dry

★ **Superstar ingredient:** Argan oil is a great natural moisturizer because it absorbs easily, is non-greasy and won't irritate your skin.

- Glass jar with lid

⅓ cup	aloe vera gel (see Top tips, page 82)	75 mL
⅓ cup	liquid vegetable glycerin (see Did you know?, opposite)	75 mL
1 tbsp	argan or marula oil	15 mL

1. Pour aloe vera gel, vegetable glycerin and argan oil into jar. Shake vigorously until well combined.

2. Using fingers, gently massage a small amount of cleanser onto damp facial skin, using circular motions.

3. Rinse face with warm water and pat dry with a towel. Follow with your favorite toner, serum and moisturizer.

4. Store at room temperature for up to 6 months.

DID YOU KNOW?

Marula oil is a new darling that's becoming as popular as argan oil. It's hydrating, it fights aging, and it's loaded with antioxidants, and omega-6 and omega-9 essential fatty acids.

The 411 on Facial Cleansers

There are three types of facial cleansers. Choose the one that caters to the needs of your skin:

1. **Water-based.** These are mild and suited to dry, sensitive or mature skin.

2. **Soap-based.** A heavier-duty option, these are best for normal, oily or combo skin.

3. **Oil-based.** These are concentrated, moisturizing, nutrient-dense formulas that are great for removing stubborn makeup on all skin types.

Gentle Rose Water Cleanser

One of the best things about rose water is that it's suitable for all types of skin. It's balancing, toning, soothing and moisturizing; plus, it's antibacterial, antiseptic and anti-inflammatory. And it smells heavenly!

Best for:

▲ Dry, ◆ Sensitive and ■ Mature skin

★ **Superstar ingredient:** Rose water has moisturizing and antibacterial properties. It balances your skin's natural pH, and can help fight acne, dermatitis and eczema.

- *Glass jar with lid*

⅓ cup	rose water	75 mL
⅓ cup	liquid vegetable glycerin	75 mL
¼ cup	aloe vera gel (see Top tips, page 82)	60 mL
1 tbsp	witch hazel (see Superstar ingredient, page 242)	15 mL

1. Pour rose water, vegetable glycerin, aloe vera gel and witch hazel into jar. Shake vigorously until well combined.

2. Using fingers, gently massage a small amount of cleanser onto damp facial skin, using circular motions.

3. Rinse face with warm water and pat dry with a towel. Follow with your favorite toner, serum and moisturizer.

4. Store in the refrigerator for up to 2 weeks.

DID YOU KNOW? Glycerin can be synthetic, animal-derived (made from tallow) or vegetable-derived (made from palm, soybean or coconut oil). You can typically find liquid vegetable glycerin online and at health food stores.

Simple Castile Soap Cleanser for Acne-Prone Skin

This basic face wash is super-easy to whip up, and it requires only two (yes, two!) main ingredients. The essential oils you choose change the formula to suit your skin.

Best for:

● Oily/acne-prone skin

TOP TIP: You'll find places to buy all my favorite essential oils in the Resources section (page 263).

★ Superstar ingredient: Liquid castile soap is a nontoxic, multipurpose concentrate made from plant oils. It can be used to clean almost anything, such as hands, body, dishes, bathrooms, counters, cars and floors.

- *Small funnel*
- *Glass soap pump dispenser*

½ cup	unscented liquid castile soap	125 mL
½ cup	filtered water	125 mL
10	drops tea tree essential oil (see info, page 73)	10
10	drops peppermint essential oil	10
10	drops lemon essential oil (see info, page 132)	10
10	drops orange essential oil (see info, page 130)	10

1. Using funnel, pour castile soap, filtered water, and tea tree, peppermint, lemon and orange essential oils into soap pump dispenser. Shake vigorously until well combined.

2. Using cotton round or fingers, gently massage a small amount of cleanser onto damp facial skin, using circular motions.

3. Rinse face with warm water and pat dry with a towel. Follow with your favorite toner and moisturizer.

4. Store at room temperature out of direct sunlight for up to 2 months.

Variations

Simple Castile Soap Cleanser for Mature Skin
Omit tea tree, peppermint, lemon and orange essential oils. Add 10 drops of frankincense, myrrh or cypress essential oil to soap mixture before shaking. Do not use myrrh essential oil if you are or might be pregnant.

Simple Castile Soap Cleanser for Dry Skin
Omit tea tree, peppermint, lemon and orange essential oils. Add 10 drops of jasmine, lavender or ylang-ylang essential oil to soap mixture before shaking. (See Caution, page 126.)

Basic Oil Cleanser for Normal Skin

So what's this trendy oil-cleansing method (OCM) all about? It sounds crazy counterintuitive, but this process uses oils — instead of soap or water — to dissolve built-up, hardened oils on your face that have clogged your pores. It may take a bit of getting used to, but once you get the hang of the OCM, it's life-changing. Trust me.

Best for:

● Normal skin

TOP TIP: Always purchase organic oils that have been cold- or expeller-pressed. They are free of toxins and chock-full of nutrients.

★ Superstar ingredient: Castor oil is a powerful antibacterial agent, and has strong cleansing, healing and anti-inflammatory properties. It's especially great for acne-prone skin.

- Glass jar with lid

1 cup	castor or sunflower oil	250 mL
3 tbsp	jojoba oil (see info, page 65)	45 mL

1. In a medium bowl, stir castor oil with jojoba oil until blended. Spoon into jar.

2. Using fingers, gently massage a small amount of oil over dry, unwashed facial skin, using circular motions.

3. Using a warm, wet washcloth, gently remove excess oil from face.

4. Store at room temperature out of direct sunlight for up to 6 months.

Variations

Basic Oil Cleanser for Dry Skin
Substitute the same amount of avocado oil for the jojoba oil.

Basic Oil Cleanser for Mature Skin
Substitute the same amount of apricot kernel oil for the jojoba oil.

Basic Oil Cleanser for Acne-Prone Skin
Substitute the same amount of hazelnut oil for the jojoba oil.

DID YOU KNOW?
There are no one-size-fits-all remedies. If this or one of the variations on this page doesn't work perfectly for your skin, experiment with different oil blends until you find a combo that makes your face happy.

Acne-Away Cleanser

Zits are the pits. Out of nowhere, these suckers show up — totally uninvited — and take up prime real estate on your pretty mug. Suddenly, it feels like everyone and her dog is staring at your problem spots. Fret not! This cleanser will help pave the path to clear skin. Zits, we've got one thing to say to you: buh-bye!

Best for:

◆ Oily/acne-prone skin

★ **Superstar ingredient:** Tea tree essential oil has powerful antibacterial properties. It makes a great natural alternative to benzoyl peroxide, the super-drying chemical used in most store-bought acne treatments.

- Glass jar with lid

½ cup	unscented liquid castile soap (see Superstar ingredient, page 70)	125 mL
1 tbsp	jojoba oil (see info, page 65)	15 mL
10	drops tea tree essential oil	10

1. Pour castile soap, jojoba oil and tea tree essential oil into jar. Shake vigorously until well combined.

2. Using fingers, gently massage a small amount of cleanser onto damp facial skin, using circular motions.

3. Rinse face with warm water and pat dry with a towel. Follow with your favorite toner, serum and moisturizer.

4. Store at room temperature out of direct sunlight for up to 6 months.

DID YOU KNOW?

Tea tree essential oil has so many antibacterial and antifungal benefits that it was commonly added to first-aid kits for Australian soldiers and sailors who served in subtropical climates during World War II. Tea tree essential oil was also commonly used in field hospitals to keep wounds from becoming infected.

Basic Toner for All Skin Types

Y'all, it's time to get toned! Don't worry, I'm not talking about squats and situps — I'm referring to that beautiful face of yours. With just a few spritzies of this simple facial toner, you'll feel clean and refreshed, all while smelling like a rose garden in full bloom.

Best for:

♥ All skin types

★ **Superstar ingredient:** Geranium essential oil can help treat acne, reduce inflammation and lift your mood. In this toner, it's a key ingredient to ensure good hydration.

- Glass spray bottle

1 cup	rose water (see Superstar ingredient, page 69)	250 mL
10	drops geranium essential oil	10

1. Pour rose water and geranium essential oil into bottle. Shake vigorously until well combined.

2. With eyes closed, spray toner a few times all over cleansed facial skin. Let dry. Follow with your favorite serum and moisturizer.

3. Store in the refrigerator for up to 1 month.

Toners

Toners are absolutely fantastic, and I feel like people often underestimate their role in facial cleansing. You know how sometimes you use a cleanser and afterward your face feels tight and thirsty? Toners are like a nice, long drink of water for your skin. Toners bring it back to a state of homeostasis, or balance.

DID YOU KNOW?
Geranium is sometimes called the "poor man's rose." The two flowers share nearly the same therapeutic traits, but geranium is way more affordable.

Pore-Shrinking Basil Toner

Sure, basil rocks the socks off Italian pasta, but here's a fave beauty secret: it shrinks the appearance of pores, too. Let's face it — enlarged pores look scary, so this toner makes a huge diff.

Best for:

● Oily/acne-prone and ■ Mature skin

★ Superstar ingredient: Basil is antioxidant-rich, anti-inflammatory, antibacterial, soothing and healing. In other words, it will tame redness, reduce acne breakouts and fight wrinkles. These are all beautiful things!

- *Mortar and pestle*
- *Fine-mesh sieve*
- *Glass spray bottle*

20	fresh basil leaves	20
½ cup	boiling water	125 mL
	Freshly squeezed lemon juice	

1. In mortar, mash basil leaves until juicy. Pour in boiling water and let stand for 5 to 10 minutes.

2. Place fine-mesh sieve over a jar or small bowl. Strain basil mixture into jar, pressing with fingers to extract as much liquid as possible. Discard soilds. Let cool.

3. Add a small squeeze of lemon juice and stir to combine. Pour into bottle.

4. With eyes closed, spray toner a few times all over cleansed facial skin. Let dry. Follow with your favorite serum or moisturizer.

5. Store in the refrigerator for up to 2 weeks.

Toner for Acne-Prone Skin

This refreshing, pH-balancing toner helps stop pimples before they rear their ugly heads. It'll seriously help your skin chill the $%#@ out. I promise I say that with a copious amount of love.

Best for:

● Oily/acne-prone skin

TOP TIP: If you don't want to use a spray bottle, you can store the toner in a glass jar with a lid. Apply the toner to cleansed facial skin with a cotton ball or round. Make sure to keep the jar in the fridge.

★ **Superstar ingredients:** Green tea is anti-inflammatory and helps with redness and blemishes, while the acid in the cider vinegar returns the skin's pH to a normal level.

- *Glass spray bottle*

1 cup	cooled brewed green tea	250 mL
¼ cup	cider vinegar	60 mL
5	drops lavender essential oil	5

1. Pour green tea, cider vinegar and lavender essential oil into bottle. Shake until well combined.

2. With eyes closed, spray toner a few times all over cleansed facial skin. Let dry. Follow with your favorite serum and moisturizer.

3. Store in the refrigerator for up to 2 weeks.

DID YOU KNOW? The lavender essential oil in this toner also helps melt away stress.

5 ALL-NATURAL DIY ZIT ZAPPERS

Acne, blemishes, spots, zits — whatever you call 'em — are goners. We're going to annihilate every last one, but in a gentle, eco-friendly, earthy-crunchy way. That's right, Retin-A and benzoyl peroxide, we don't need you. Later, suckers! You can use any or all of these treatments, picking and choosing which ones you like best:

1. **Steam + Aspirin.** Hold your face over a bowl filled with boiling filtered water, and let the steam prime your pores. Then, crush an Aspirin tablet and mix it with a few drops of water to form a paste. Apply that paste to every pesky pimply spot and let it stand for 5 minutes. Rinse your face off and pat it dry with a towel. The Aspirin will help reduce inflammation and redness.

2. **Lemon + salt.** Mix 2 tsp (10 mL) of freshly squeezed lemon juice with a pinch of salt and apply to your acne-affected areas. Let it stand on your skin for 15 to 20 minutes. Rinse your face off and pat it dry with a towel. Lemon is an astringent and will zap that oil right off your face.

3. **Cider vinegar.** Dab a bit of cider vinegar on your spotty areas and leave it on overnight. This treatment has a bit of a stank factor, so apologize to your honey-bunny in advance before hitting the hay. Rinse it off in the morning and pat your skin dry with a towel.

4. **Witch hazel.** Soak a cotton ball in witch hazel (another all-natural astringent) and generously apply it to zits. Let it air-dry.

5. **Garlic.** Okay, I saved the stinkiest remedy for last (you're welcome). Did you know garlic is a zit-zapping wonder? It's antiseptic and antibacterial. Smash one clove of garlic and mix it with $\frac{1}{3}$ cup (75 mL) of warm water. Apply the mixture to your face and let it stand for 3 to 5 minutes. Rinse your face off and pat it dry with a towel.

Rose Water Toner for Dry or Sensitive Skin

When rose season comes around, take advantage of your garden or the flower section of your local organic supermarket, and make your very own refreshing, floral, rosy face mist. Rose water is awesome because it smells ah-mazing, and it's great for dry, sensitive skin.

Best for:

▲ Dry and
◆ Sensitive skin

TOP TIP: Make sure you get your paws on roses that haven't been sprayed with pesticides, herbicides or anything else toxic. You don't want those chemicals on your face!

★ Superstar ingredient: Roses contain approximately 275 compounds that have a myriad of therapeutic uses, from helping to banish eczema, wrinkles and acne to naturally lifting your mood to helping you sleep better.

- *Fine-mesh sieve*
- *Glass spray bottle*

| 1 cup | unsprayed rose petals, rinsed and drained | 250 mL |
| 2 cups | boiling filtered water | 500 mL |

1. Place rose petals in a large heatproof glass bowl. Pour boiling water over petals and cover tightly. Let stand for 3 to 4 hours.

2. Place sieve over a large bowl. Strain rose water into bowl, discarding solids. Pour rose water into bottle.

3. With eyes closed, spray toner a few times all over cleansed facial skin. Let dry. Follow with your favorite moisturizer.

4. Store in the refrigerator for up to 2 weeks.

Lovely Lavender Fresh-Face Spray

Feeling frazzled? Spritz on this potion to boost your mood, soothe anxiety and defuse stress. Keep a bottle at work and at home.

Best for:

♥ All skin types

TOP TiPS: Aloe vera juice is not the same as aloe vera gel. The juice is super-liquidy and found just under the skin of the plant's leaves; the gel comes from the fleshy inner core of the leaves. You can buy aloe vera juice and gel at health food stores.

You can use this spray as a skin-freshening pick-me-up throughout the day.

★ Superstar ingredient: Lavender has calming properties that help you de-stress, calm jangly nerves and ease mild depression.

• *Glass spray bottle*

½ cup	coconut water	125 mL
½ cup	aloe vera juice	125 mL
15 to 20	drops lavender essential oil	15 to 20

1. Pour coconut water, aloe vera juice and lavender essential oil into bottle. Shake vigorously until well combined.

2. With eyes closed, spray mixture a few times all over cleansed facial skin. Let dry. Follow with your favorite serum or moisturizer.

3. Store in the refrigerator for up to 1 month.

Gentle Antiaging Toner

If you're looking to fight the visible signs of aging (that's me, for sure), look no further than chamomile tea. Besides being mad-tasty and soothing as a drink, it also reduces redness, blemishes and irritation when applied to the skin. It's loaded with antioxidants that help fight free radicals, which are the culprits behind those dreaded wrinkles.

Best for:

♥ All skin types, especially ■ Mature

TOP TiP: If you don't want to use a spray bottle, you can store the toner in a glass jar with a lid. Apply the toner to cleansed facial skin with a cotton ball or round. Make sure to keep the jar in the fridge.

★ Superstar ingredient:

Chamomile is antibacterial, antifungal, anti-inflammatory and antiseptic. It's also hypoallergenic, making it gentle for people with sensitive skin.

- *Glass spray bottle*

1 cup	cooled brewed chamomile tea	250 mL
½ cup	aloe vera gel (see Top tips, opposite)	125 mL
10	drops clary sage essential oil (see Caution, below)	10

1. Pour chamomile tea, aloe vera gel and clary sage essential oil into bottle. Shake until well combined.

2. With eyes closed, spray toner a few times all over cleansed facial skin. Let dry. Follow with your favorite serum and moisturizer.

3. Store in the refrigerator for up to 2 weeks.

Caution: Don't use sage or clary sage in any form if you are pregnant or nursing, or have epilepsy.

Zit-Zapping Blemish Stick

Zits! We all have to work around these nasty blemishes, and it can suck. Treating them with some all-natural goodness and TLC can work wonders, whether you're dealing with teenage acne or a hormonal flare-up. BTW, don't freak when you see all the oils that go into this recipe — these were specifically chosen because they are acne-fighting, skin-balancing oils that *won't* clog pores.

Best for:

⬥ Oily/acne-prone skin

TOP TIPS: Cocoa butter usually comes in big ol' chunks (sometimes in chip form, too). To measure it, you need to grate it first. Use a rasp grater or the fine side of a box grater.

If you don't want to melt your wax or butter mixture in a heatproof bowl over simmering water, you can microwave it on High, stirring every 10 seconds, until it's melted and completely smooth. The total time will depend on the strength of your microwave.

★ Superstar ingredient: Tea tree essential oil is a healthy, natural alternative to expensive, unnatural, chemical-laden acne treatments you can buy in stores.

- *3 lip balm tubes*

1 tbsp	candelilla wax (see Top tip, page 160)	15 mL
¾ tsp	grated cocoa butter	3 mL
¾ tsp	castor oil (see Superstar ingredient, page 72)	3 mL
¾ tsp	vitamin E oil (see Did you know?, page 214)	3 mL
¾ tsp	tea tree essential oil	3 mL
¾ tsp	peppermint essential oil (see Did you know?, page 123)	3 mL
¾ tsp	lavender essential oil (see Superstar ingredient, page 82)	3 mL

1. Place candelilla wax and cocoa butter in a small metal or heatproof glass bowl. Pour enough water into a small saucepan to come about 1½ inches (4 cm) up the side; bring to a simmer. Place bowl on saucepan, making sure the bottom doesn't touch the water. Heat, stirring, for 5 to 10 minutes or until wax mixture is melted and smooth.

2. Stir in castor oil, vitamin E oil, and tea tree, peppermint and lavender essential oils.

3. Pour oil mixture into lip balm tubes. Let cool completely.

4. Apply stick directly to trouble spots after cleansing and toning.

5. Store at room temperature out of direct sunlight for up to 6 months.

DID YOU KNOW?

The practice of using tea tree essential oil started in Australia. For thousands of years, the Aborigine community has used it to cure cuts, burns and boils, and as an antiseptic.

Potent Antiaging Rose Serum

Turn back the clock with this rich serum. It will give you a dewy, fresh-faced glow!

Best for:

♥ All skin types, especially ■ Mature

TOP TiP: Rose essential oil is mad-expensive — I've seen a teensy $1/8$-oz (3.7 mL) bottle retail for as much as $75! That's because it takes 60 roses to make *one* drop of pure rose essential oil. Whoa. So that's why we're using just one drop for this recipe.

- Small glass bottle with eyedropper top

2 tbsp	avocado oil (see Superstar ingredient, page 160)	30 mL
1	drop rose essential oil (see Caution, below)	1
5	drops frankincense essential oil	5

1. In a small bowl, stir together avocado oil, rose essential oil and frankincense essential oil until well combined. Pour into bottle.

2. Using eyedropper, place 5 to 10 drops of serum all over dry cleansed facial skin. Using fingers, gently massage skin until serum is absorbed.

3. Store in a cool, dark place for up to 6 months.

Caution: Do not use rose essential oil if you are or might be pregnant.

DID YOU KNOW? Rose essential oil reduces the appearance of skin imperfections and evens out skin tone. Plus, it smells be-YOU-tee-ful, am I right?

Customizable Hemp Seed Facial Oil

Hemp seed oil is seriously becoming a favorite beauty staple of mine. It works well as an anti-inflammatory, non-greasy moisturizer, and it's ideal for all skin types. Whatever your skin needs, you can make this recipe work for you. Different essential oils are the key to creating the perfect formula to suit your beautiful face.

Best for:

♥ All skin types

TOP TIP: The final essential oil you're adding to this formula will be determined by which type of skin you have. Lavender essential oil is great for all skin types. Use geranium essential oil if you have sensitive skin. Use lemon essential oil for dry skin. For acne-prone skin, use rosemary essential oil (see Caution, page 91). And for mature skin, use frankincense essential oil.

★ **Superstar ingredient:** Hemp seed oil is magical. It's a dry oil, meaning it soaks in fast and doesn't leave any greasy residue. Plus, it scores 0 on the comedogenic scale (see page 47), so it won't clog your pores and cause nasty blackheads.

Caution: Do not use carrot seed essential oil if you are or might be pregnant.

- Small funnel
- Glass bottle with eyedropper top

¼ cup	hemp seed oil	60 mL
2 tbsp	jojoba oil (see info, page 65)	30 mL
1 tbsp	grapeseed oil (see info, page 111)	15 mL
1 tsp	carrot seed essential oil (see Caution, below)	5 mL
10 to 15	drops skin type–specific essential oil	10 to 15

1. In a small bowl, stir together hemp seed oil, jojoba oil, grapeseed oil, carrot seed essential oil and skin type–specific essential oil until well combined. Using funnel, pour into bottle.

2. Using eyedropper, place 5 to 10 drops of oil all over dry cleansed facial skin. Using fingers, gently massage skin until oil is absorbed.

3. Store in the refrigerator for up to 6 months.

DID YOU KNOW?

Hemp seed oil shrinks the appearance of pores, acts as an anti-inflammatory and is chock-full of essential fatty acids. Always keep hemp seed oil in the fridge once it's opened, to keep it from spoiling.

Kick-Ass Wake-Up Coffee Serum

Coffee is loaded with anti-inflammatory caffeine, which improves the appearance of puffy under-eye bags and dark circles. Rooibos is antioxidant-rich and antibacterial, and it has been known to help with skin disorders, including eczema and acne. The coffee in this serum smells insanely delish. You've been warned.

Best for:

♥ All skin types

TOP TIPS: Save your leftover coffee-and-rooibos mixture to make Pore De-Gunking Coffee Facial Scrub (page 96).

Vanilla extract used for cooking is very different from vanilla absolute (see Did you know?, right). Save your extract for scrumptious vegan muffins and cookies.

• *Glass bottle with eyedropper top*

½ cup	sweet almond oil (see info, page 136)	125 mL
1 tbsp	avocado oil (see Superstar ingredient, page 160)	15 mL
¼ cup	ground coffee (see info, page 96)	60 mL
¼ cup	rooibos tea leaves (see Superstar ingredient, page 92)	60 mL
1 tsp	argan oil (see Superstar ingredient, page 68)	5 mL
1 tsp	vitamin E oil (see Did you know?, page 214)	5 mL
10	drops vanilla absolute	10

1. Using the Quick Heat Infusion or the Slow Cold Infusion method on page 46, infuse sweet almond oil and avocado oil with ground coffee and rooibos tea. Strain as directed.

2. In a small bowl, stir together infusion, argan oil, vitamin E oil and vanilla absolute until well combined. Pour into bottle.

3. Using eyedropper, place 5 to 10 drops of serum all over dry cleansed facial skin after applying toner. Using fingers, gently massage skin until serum is absorbed.

4. Store in a cool, dark place for up to 6 months.

DID YOU KNOW? The only way to capture the yummy aroma of the vanilla bean is to use a solvent; the concentrated oil produced by combining a solvent with a plant is called an absolute. If you see a product labeled vanilla essential oil, it's usually just vanilla extract diluted with a carrier oil, such as jojoba (read: false advertising).

Miracle Antiaging Night Cream

You guys, this night cream is everything! It's potent, way more so than store-bought versions made with junky fillers. And I speak from personal experience when I say it totally works. This stuff keeps my skin supple and youthful. It's almost too good to share.

Best for:

♥ All skin types, especially ■ Mature

★ **Superstar ingredient:** Rose hip seed oil is rich in vitamins, essential fatty acids and antioxidants (such as tretinoin and beta-carotene). These antioxidants have been shown to help correct dark spots; hydrate dry, itchy skin; fight wrinkles; and improve skin texture and tone. Rose hip seed oil is also non-greasy and super-light, which is why I like to slather it on my whole face before I go beddy-bye.

- *Blender*
- *Small glass jar with lid*

1 tsp	candelilla wax (see Top tip, page 160)	5 mL
½ tsp	shea butter (see Caution, page 220)	2 mL
1 tsp	coconut oil (see info, page 170)	5 mL
½ tsp	argan or marula oil (see info, page 68)	2 mL
½ tsp	rose hip seed oil	2 mL
¼ tsp	vitamin E oil (see Did you know?, page 214)	1 mL
10	drops rosemary essential oil (see Caution, below)	10

1. Place candelilla wax and shea butter in a small heatproof glass bowl (see Top tips, page 84). Pour enough water into a small saucepan to come about 1½ inches (4 cm) up the side; bring to a simmer. Place bowl on saucepan, making sure the bottom doesn't touch the water. Heat, stirring, for 5 to 10 minutes or until wax mixture is melted and smooth.

2. Remove bowl from heat. Stir in coconut oil, argan oil, rose hip seed oil, vitamin E oil and rosemary essential oil. Transfer to blender and blend until smooth and creamy. Pour into jar.

3. Using fingers, spread cream over toned cleansed facial skin before going to bed.

4. Store in a cool, dark place for up to 6 months.

Caution: Do not use rosemary essential oil if you are or might be pregnant.

Creamy Dreamy Rooibos Moisturizer

Rooibos is my all-time fave tea. It's delicately sweet and caffeine-free. Yum! There was absolutely no way I was going to write this book without including a rooibos beauty recipe — or a few of them.

Best for:

♥ All skin types

★ **Superstar ingredient:** Rooibos is packed with antioxidants and minerals. It's also naturally hypoallergenic and antibacterial.

• *Glass jar with lid*

1 cup	sweet almond oil (see info, page 136)	250 mL
1 cup	rooibos tea leaves	250 mL
2 tbsp	candelilla wax (see Top tip, page 160)	30 mL
10	drops argan oil (see Superstar ingredient, page 68)	10
5	drops vitamin E oil (see Did you know?, page 214)	5

1. Using the Quick Heat Infusion or the Slow Cold Infusion method on page 46, infuse sweet almond oil with rooibos tea. Strain as directed.

2. Place candelilla wax in a medium metal or heatproof glass bowl (see Top tips, page 84). Pour enough water into a medium saucepan to come about 1½ inches (4 cm) up the side; bring to a simmer. Place bowl on saucepan, making sure the bottom doesn't touch the water. Heat, stirring, for 5 to 10 minutes or until wax is melted and smooth.

3. Remove bowl from heat. Stir in infusion, argan oil and vitamin E oil. Pour into jar. Let cool completely until solid.

4. Using fingers, spread moisturizer all over toned cleansed facial skin twice a day.

5. Store in a cool, dark place for up to 6 months.

Basic Facial Scrub

It's no secret that I'm obsessed with cleansing scrubs. Salt-based, sugar-based, baking soda–based — I need 'em all because dead skin cells aren't welcome on this face.

Best for:

♥ All skin types

TOP TiPS: Use kaolin or French green clay in this recipe if you have dry or sensitive skin. Swap in rhassoul or fuller's earth clay for oily skin.

One ingredient I'm totally not OK with in store-bought scrubs is microbeads. Those tiny bits of evil plastic are used as exfoliants in facial and body scrubs, and even toothpastes. Microbeads mega-suck because they're so teensy that sewage treatment plants can't keep them from sneaking into bodies of water. Poor Mama Earth! That's just one more reason we're gonna rock the DIY facial scrubs in this chapter.

2 tsp	finely ground rolled oats (see info, opposite)	10 mL
1 tsp	baking soda	5 mL
1 tsp	clay	5 mL
	Water or jojoba oil	

1. In a small bowl, stir together oats, baking soda and clay until well combined.

2. Scoop a small amount into palm and add enough water to make a paste.

3. Using fingers, gently spread scrub all over damp cleansed facial skin, using circular motions.

4. Rinse face with warm water and pat dry with a towel. Follow with your favorite toner and moisturizer.

DID YOU KNOW?
Baking soda is great at buffing away dead skin cells. It also has antiseptic properties, so it slays zit-causing bacteria. It's an ideal ingredient for people with acne-prone skin.

Not-So-Basic Facial Scrub

Actually, this scrub is still pretty basic. Oats are great, not only for breakfast noms but also for exfoliating skin like nobody's business. (Only thing better is when they posse up with cornmeal.) Oats effectively absorb and remove dirt and impurities that are slumming around on your skin.

Best for:

♥ All skin types

TOP TIP: If your cornmeal is too coarse, just dump it in your food processor and whizz it around two or three times until it's superfine.

★ **Superstar ingredient:** Oats can be both soothing and moisturizing, which is crucial after some down-and-dirty scrubby action. Oats are anti-inflammatory and emollient, too, which means they soften and hydrate your skin.

3 tbsp	finely ground rolled oats	45 mL
2 tbsp	sweet almond oil (see info, page 136)	30 mL
1 tbsp	superfine cornmeal	15 mL
1 tbsp	agave syrup	15 mL

1. In a small bowl, stir together oats, sweet almond oil, cornmeal and agave syrup until dry ingredients are moistened.

2. Using fingers, spread scrub all over damp cleansed facial skin, using circular motions. Let stand on skin for 5 minutes.

3. Rinse face with warm water and pat dry with a towel. Follow with your favorite toner, serum and moisturizer.

DID YOU KNOW? Mucilage, a gelatinous combination of protein and carbohydrates, in oats retains water and is responsible for working some moisturizing magic on your face.

Pore De-Gunking Coffee Facial Scrub

All right, all you coffee fiends, let's put those coffee grounds to use on your faces! Coffee wakes you up, yes, but it's also a kick-ass exfoliant. It sloughs off dry, crusty, dead skin (gross but true), and it smells *so* good. The caffeine in the beans helps treat redness and inflammation, and decreases the appearance of under-eye circles.

Best for:

♥ All skin types

TOP TIP: You don't need to grind coffee beans specially for this recipe. Feel free to use the leftover grounds from your morning cup-o'-joe. Or sub in the coffee-and-rooibos combo leftover from making a batch of Kick-Ass Wake-Up Coffee Serum (page 90). In either case, run them through a coffee or spice grinder a few times to make sure they're really fine.

★ **Superstar ingredient:** Coffee is an effective exfoliator, and the caffeine it contains tightens and tones your skin.

• Blender (optional)

2½ tsp	coconut oil (see info, page 170)	12 mL
1 tbsp	very finely ground coffee	15 mL
1½ tsp	packed fine vegan brown sugar (see Top tip, page 145)	7 mL
1 tsp	maple syrup	5 mL

1. In a small saucepan over low heat, melt coconut oil.

2. In blender, purée coconut oil, coffee, brown sugar and maple syrup until well combined and spreadable. Spoon into a small bowl. (Alternatively, in a small bowl, whisk ingredients together until smooth.)

3. Using fingers, spread scrub all over damp cleansed facial skin, using circular motions.

4. Rinse face with warm water and pat dry with a towel. Follow with your favorite toner, serum and moisturizer.

5. Cover and store any leftovers in the refrigerator for up to 1 month.

DID YOU KNOW? Maple syrup isn't just for pancakes. It's also antibacterial, nutrient-rich and moisturizing for the skin.

Hella-Bomb Oatmeal Facial Scrub

The environment is full of free radicals and pollution, both of which wreak havoc on our delicate faces. Combine those with layers of nasty dead and unwanted skin cells, and we need oatmeal to come to our rescue! This fail-safe recipe for baby booty–smooth skin allows you to have your oats and eat them, too, sans the harsh cleansers and chemical gunkies.

Best for:

♥ All skin types

TOP TiP: Almond flour is really, really finely ground blanched almonds, which don't have the skins on. You can usually find bags of it in the health food aisle at your supermarket.

★ Superstar ingredient:

Rhassoul clay reduces dryness, improves skin tone and elasticity, and has the ability to unblock pores and clear up even the most stubborn blackheads.

1 tbsp	finely ground rolled oats (see info, page 95)	15 mL
2 tsp	almond flour	10 mL
2 tsp	rhassoul clay	10 mL
5	drops lavender essential oil (see Superstar ingredient, page 82)	5
5	drops lemon essential oil (see info, page 132)	5
	Warm water	

1. In a small bowl, stir together oats, almond flour, clay, lavender essential oil and lemon essential oil until well combined. Add warm water, stirring in a few drops at a time, until a paste forms.

2. Using fingers, spread scrub all over damp cleansed facial skin, using circular motions. Let stand on skin for 5 to 10 minutes.

3. Rinse face with warm water and pat dry with a towel. Follow with your favorite toner, serum and moisturizer.

4. Cover and store any leftovers in the refrigerator for up to 2 weeks.

Fruity AHA Facial Peel

Are you ready to rock a super-easy, affordable fruity facial peel without taking a trip to a physician's office or dealing with the harsh chemicals and preservatives often found in store-bought brands? I thought so!

Best for:

♥ All skin types, except ◆ Sensitive

TOP TiPS: Papaya and pineapple are naturally high in alpha hydroxy acids (AHAs), a type of fruit acid that's popular in tons of fancy antiaging skin-care products. AHAs rejuvenate your look by encouraging the shedding of old, sun-damaged cells on the surface of your skin.

If you don't feel like peeling and coring the whole fruit, canned pineapple works just as well as fresh in this recipe.

★ **Superstar ingredients:** Papayas and pineapples are also loaded with vitamin C, which promotes collagen production in the skin. Win-win!

• *Blender or food processor*

¼ cup	cubed seeded peeled papaya	60 mL
4	chunks (about 1½ inches/4 cm) cored peeled pineapple	4
2 tsp	jojoba oil (see info, page 65)	10 mL

1. In blender, purée papaya, pineapple and jojoba oil until smooth. Spoon into a small bowl.

2. Using fingers, spread mixture all over damp cleansed facial skin, using circular motions. Let stand on skin for 10 to 15 minutes.

3. Rinse face with warm water and pat dry with a towel. Follow with your favorite toner and moisturizer.

4. Cover and store any leftovers in the refrigerator for up to 1 week.

Matcha Green Goddess Facial Mask

I'm a big-time matcha maniac. This powdered, concentrated green tea won me over even more when I read up on its metabolism-enhancing, stress-reducing, immune-boosting, cholesterol-lowering and antiaging powers. It's definitely worth sipping a cuppa when you chill with this mask on.

Best for:

- Oily/acne-prone,
- Normal and
- Combination skin

★ **Superstar ingredient:** Matcha is full of antioxidants and contains chlorophyll, a powerful detoxifier. It also has the ability to decrease sebum production, making it especially kind to acne-prone skin.

- *Blender (optional)*

3 tbsp	water	45 mL
1 tbsp	matcha powder	15 mL
½ tsp	coconut oil (see info, page 170)	2 mL
¼ tsp	freshly squeezed lemon juice	1 mL
Pinch	turmeric	Pinch

1. In blender, purée water, matcha powder, coconut oil, lemon juice and turmeric until a paste forms. Spoon into a small bowl. (Alternatively, in a small bowl, whisk ingredients together until pasty.)

2. Using fingers, spread a thin layer of mask all over damp cleansed facial skin. Let stand on skin for 10 minutes.

3. Rinse face with warm water and pat dry with a towel. Follow with your favorite toner and moisturizer.

DID YOU KNOW?
One cup of matcha has as many antioxidants as 10 cups of brewed regular green tea.

Black Forest Chocolate Cake Facial Mask

This recipe is made with such yummy ingredients, like cocoa powder and luscious ripe cherries, that you'll need serious willpower not to bake up a vegan cake to match. Oh, what the heck, why not make both? As Oscar Wilde wrote, "The only way to get rid of a temptation is to yield to it."

Best for:

♥ All skin types

TOP TIP: Cherry juice is useful for lightening skin and clearing up dark spots. Cherries contain the antioxidant vitamins A and C, plus the minerals potassium, zinc, iron, copper and manganese. The fruit and juice are anti-inflammatory, moisturizing and healing for damaged skin.

★ **Superstar ingredient:** Cocoa powder is antioxidant-rich, so it helps neutralize harmful free radicals and repair skin cells.

• *Blender*

3	large ripe cherries, pitted	3
1 tbsp	kaolin clay	15 mL
1 tbsp	almond milk	15 mL
2 tsp	unsweetened cocoa powder	10 mL

1. In blender, purée cherries, clay, almond milk and cocoa powder until smooth. Spoon into a small bowl.

2. Using fingers, spread mask all over damp cleansed facial skin. Let stand on skin for 10 minutes.

3. Rinse face with warm water and pat dry with a towel. Follow with your favorite toner and moisturizer.

4. Cover and store any leftovers in the refrigerator for up to 1 week.

Green Clay Detox Facial Mask

This simple clay mask is great for peeps with oily skin, combo skin and normal skin. Clays are antiseptic, anti-inflammatory deep cleansers that draw out impurities and toxins, leaving you looking gorgeous.

Best for:

- ◖ Oily/acne-prone,
- ● Normal and
- ◑ Combination skin

★ **Superstar ingredients:** French green clay is made of teeny molecules that are super-absorbent and literally drink oils and toxins out of your skin. The agave syrup softens and hydrates skin.

4 tsp	plain nondairy yogurt	20 mL
1 tbsp	French green clay	15 mL
½ tsp	agave syrup	2 mL

1. In a small bowl, stir together yogurt, clay and agave syrup until well combined.

2. Using fingers, spread mask all over damp cleansed facial skin. Let stand on skin for 10 minutes.

3. Rinse face with warm water and pat dry with a towel. Follow with your favorite toner and moisturizer.

DID YOU KNOW?

Nondairy yogurt has antibacterial and antifungal powers, making it great for pampering acne-prone skin. Yogurt also helps exfoliate and tightens pores with its naturally occurring lactic acid.

Skin-Quenching Facial Mask

If your skin is parched like the Sahara Desert, it's time to hook it up with a heaping moisture-intensive dose of facial-mask love. Cocoa powder contains heaps of antioxidants, increases blood flow and improves skin hydration. Plus, it's chocolate — you gotta love that!

Best for:

♥ All skin types, especially ▲ Dry

★ **Superstar ingredients:** Oats soothe irritated, dry and itchy skin. Olive oil has mega-moisturizing powers, too.

2 tbsp	olive oil	30 mL
1 tbsp	unsweetened cocoa powder	15 mL
1 tbsp	finely ground rolled oats	15 mL

1. In a small bowl, stir together olive oil, cocoa powder and oats until creamy.

2. Using fingers, spread mask all over damp cleansed facial skin. Let stand on skin for 15 minutes.

3. Rinse face with warm water and pat dry with a towel. Follow with your favorite toner and moisturizer.

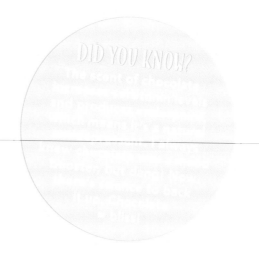

Mellow (Yellow) Out Your Skin Turmeric Facial Mask

Turmeric has anti-inflammatory, antibacterial and antioxidant properties, so it's wicked at slowing down aging and healing your skin. This mask helps keep pesky breakouts from occurring.

Best for:

● Normal, ◐ Oily/acne-prone, ■ Mature and ◑ Combination skin

★ Superstar ingredient:

Turmeric is a member of the ginger family. Yes, it's a wonderful spice for curries and tofu scrambles, but it works wonders on your skin, too. Its anti-inflammatory and antioxidant powers make it terrific for treating acne, eczema and redness (especially that caused by rosacea). Turmeric also helps soften fine lines and wrinkles.

• Blender

½	ripe banana, broken into chunks (see Did you know?, page 110)	½
1 tbsp	plain nondairy yogurt (see Did you know?, page 106)	15 mL
½ tsp	turmeric	2 mL

1. In blender, purée banana, yogurt and turmeric until smooth. Spoon into a small bowl.

2. Using fingers or a brush, spread mask all over damp cleansed facial skin. Let stand on skin for 10 minutes.

3. Rinse face with warm water, using a warm, wet washcloth to remove banana mixture. Pat dry with a towel. Follow with your favorite toner and moisturizer.

Zit-Blasting Bananarama Facial Mask

Whether you have acne-prone skin or temperamental (and possibly hormonal) flare-ups, this mask will be your new BFM (best facial mask). Once you've mashed it up, take a big ol' whiff: this mask smells and looks a bit like banana pudding. Yum!

Best for:

● Oily/acne-prone skin

★ Superstar ingredients:

This mask contains a symphony of healthful ingredients. Bananas are rich in vitamins B_6 and C. Jojoba oil helps unclog pores and controls surplus sebum production. Lemon juice is an astringent that tightens pores and brightens and evens skin tone. And turmeric has antioxidant and anti-inflammatory properties that'll help keep annoying acne spots at bay.

⅓	large ripe banana	⅓
1 tsp	castor oil or jojoba oil	5 mL
5	drops freshly squeezed lemon juice	5
Pinch	turmeric	Pinch

1. In a small bowl, using a fork, mash together banana, castor oil, lemon juice and turmeric until smooth.

2. Using fingers, spread mask all over damp cleansed facial skin. Let stand on skin for 15 minutes.

3. Rinse face with warm water and pat dry with a towel. Follow with your favorite toner and moisturizer.

4. Cover and store any leftovers in the refrigerator for up to 1 week.

DID YOU KNOW?
Sure, they make a good breakfast, but bananas also soothe and exfoliate skin. Double duty!

Party Like It's 1999 Antiaging Facial Mask

Looking to turn back the hands of time? It's never too early to start fighting wrinkles and fine lines. This yummy facial mask is packed with essential fatty acids, vitamins and anti-inflammatory components. Who knew the fountain of youth was in your kitchen?

Best for:

♥ All skin types, especially ▲ Dry and ■ Mature

★ Superstar ingredient:

Grapeseed oil is rich in vitamin E and essential fatty acids. It's an excellent moisturizer. Plus, it's great for treating acne, tightening skin and banishing dark circles around the eyes.

2 tbsp	coarsely chopped peeled pitted ripe avocado (see Superstar ingredient, page 112)	30 mL
1 tbsp	grapeseed oil	15 mL
3 to 5	drops vitamin E oil (see Did you know?, page 214)	3 to 5

1. In a small bowl, using a fork, mash together avocado, grapeseed oil and vitamin E oil.

2. Using fingers, spread mask all over dry cleansed facial skin. Let stand on skin for 10 to 15 minutes.

3. Rinse face with warm water and pat dry with a towel. Follow with your favorite toner and moisturizer.

DID YOU KNOW? Grapeseed oil is considered a dry oil. This means it is absorbed into the skin quickly and won't leave a greasy feeling behind.

Avocado Banana Skin-Soothing Smoothie Facial Mask

Here are two of my favorite things to do in the kitchen: 1) make vegan skin-care recipes, and 2) eat and drink the leftovers. This mask makes you beautiful and revs you up with plant-based energy.

Best for:

♥ All skin types

TOP TIP: Add ½ cup (125 mL) of ice to this recipe and blend to make a delicious and nutritious smoothie.

★ **Superstar ingredient:** Avocados are packed with vitamins and healthy fats that work wonders on people who have acne, as well as those who have sensitive or dry skin.

• *Blender*

1	small ripe banana (see Did you know?, page 110)	1
½	ripe avocado	½
1 tbsp	plain nondairy yogurt	15 mL
1 tsp	freshly squeezed lemon juice	5 mL
1 tsp	agave syrup	5 mL
	Fresh basil leaves	

1. Remove the pit from avocado. Cube and scoop out the flesh. Discard peel.

2. In blender, purée banana, avocado, yogurt, lemon juice and agave syrup until smooth. Add basil leaves to taste. Purée until smooth and creamy. Spoon into a small bowl.

3. Using fingers, spread mask all over damp cleansed facial skin. Let stand on skin for 10 minutes.

4. Rinse face with warm water and pat dry with a towel. Follow with your favorite toner and moisturizer.

5. Cover and store any leftovers in the refrigerator for 3 to 5 days.

What's a Smoothie Facial Mask?

All of my smoothie masks (here and on pages 115 and 116) are packed with vitamins and minerals that are good for you inside and out. In each recipe, you'll find a tip that will help you transform the mask into a delicious, nutrient-packed smoothie. Beauty never tasted sooooooooo good!

Antioxidant Blueberry Delight Smoothie Facial Mask

Blueberries are delicious and good for you. Plus, they fight free radicals and keep your face radiant and youthful-looking. The only thing that makes this smoothie mask better is if you use farm-fresh organic blueberries to make it.

Best for:

♥ All skin types, especially ■ Mature

TOP TiP: Add 1 cup (250 mL) each of nut milk and ice, and 1 frozen banana to this recipe and blend for a satisfying, yummy-in-your-tummy smoothie.

★ **Superstar ingredient:** The deep blue color of blueberries comes from compounds called anthocyanins, powerful antioxidants that protect the skin from free radicals. The vitamin C in blueberries helps the body produce collagen, while the phytonutrients (plant compounds) in them can help protect against skin cancer. Amazing, right?

• Blender

1 cup	fresh blueberries	250 mL
1	package (8 oz/250 g) plain nondairy yogurt (see Did you know?, page 106)	1

1. In blender, purée blueberries with yogurt until almost smooth and creamy. (Some chunks are OK.) Spoon into a small bowl.

2. Using fingers, spread mask all over damp cleansed facial skin. Let stand on skin for 10 minutes.

3. Rinse face with warm water and pat dry with a towel. Follow with your favorite toner and moisturizer.

4. Cover and store any leftovers in the refrigerator for up to 1 week.

DID YOU KNOW?
Blueberries improve your circulation, which makes your skin glow.

Just-Glow-with-It Spinach Smoothie Facial Mask

Popeye was right: spinach is the food you should be eating ... and using in your beauty regimen. This dark leafy green nourishes you with protein, vitamins and minerals, giving you that healthy sparkle. You glow, girl!

Best for:

♥ All skin types

TOP TiP: Add ½ cup (125 mL) of ice to this recipe and blend for a delish green smoothie.

★ **Superstar ingredient:** Spinach is packed with antioxidants, beta-carotene, vitamins C and E, manganese, selenium and zinc.

- Blender

1	handful baby spinach leaves	1
1	ripe banana (see Did you know?, page 110)	1
1 tbsp	agave syrup	15 mL
1 tsp	hemp seed oil	5 mL

1. In blender, purée spinach, banana, agave syrup and hemp seed oil until smooth and creamy. Spoon into a small bowl.

2. Using fingers or a brush, spread mask all over damp cleansed facial skin. Let stand on skin for 10 minutes.

3. Rinse face with warm water and pat dry with a towel. Follow with your favorite toner and moisturizer.

4. Cover and store any leftovers in the refrigerator for up to 1 week.

DID YOU KNOW? Hemp seed oil increases blood circulation and fights wrinkles and acne.

Sunny's Homemade Sunscreen

Even though my name is Sunny, I'm totally like a vampire when it comes to sunshiny rays. I love getting vitamin D from the sun, but I know too much exposure can cause brown age spots, dilated blood vessels, wrinkles and skin cancer. No, thanks. Sunscreen with adequate SPF is essential, people, but it's gotta be natural.

Best for:

♥ All skin types

TOP TIPS: Non-nano zinc oxide is made without any nasty nanoparticles. Our bodies aren't designed to deal with these itty bitty, teeny weeny, potentially toxic substances that manage to infiltrate our skin's protective barrier.

This sunscreen is not waterproof, so you'll need to reapply after sweating or swimming.

- *Hand mixer*
- *Glass jar with lid*

¼ cup	shea butter (see Caution, page 220)	60 mL
2 tbsp	candelilla wax (see Top tip, page 160)	30 mL
¼ cup	coconut oil (see info, page 170)	60 mL
2 tbsp	avocado oil	30 mL
2 tsp	non-nano zinc oxide (optional)	10 mL
1 tsp	red raspberry seed oil	5 mL
1 tsp	carrot seed essential oil (see Caution, page 88)	5 mL

1. In a small metal or heatproof glass bowl, combine shea butter and candelilla wax (see Top tips, page 84). Pour enough water into a small saucepan to come about 1½ inches (4 cm) up the side; bring to a simmer. Place bowl on saucepan, making sure the bottom doesn't touch the water. Heat, stirring, for 5 to 10 minutes or until shea butter mixture is melted and smooth.

2. Stir in coconut oil and avocado oil. Heat, stirring, for 2 to 3 minutes.

3. Remove bowl from heat and refrigerate for 30 minutes.

4. Remove bowl from refrigerator. Using hand mixer, beat in zinc oxide (if using), red raspberry seed oil and carrot seed essential oil for 2 minutes or until fluffy. Spoon into jar.

5. Using fingers, rub sunscreen all over face and body before sun exposure.

6. Store in the refrigerator for up to 1 year.

DID YOU KNOW? If you simply skip the zinc oxide (which is optional), you have yourself a luxe antiaging body cream that just happens have an SPF of 40 to 50.

TOXIC SUNSCREENS

The EWG recently reviewed more than 2,000 sunscreens made by more than 257 brands. You know what they found? More than 75% of those sunscreens contained toxic chemicals that can actually *increase* your risk of cancer. Increase! Doesn't that defeat the purpose of sunscreen?

TOXIC CHEMICALS FOUND IN CONVENTIONAL SUNSCREENS

These are the nasties you need to steer clear of in your sun-care regimen:

- Dioxybenzone
- Homosalate
- Menthyl anthranilate
- Methoxycinnamate (octinoxate)
- Octocrylene
- Octyl salicylate (octisalate)
- Oxybenzone
- Para-aminobenzoic acid (PABA)
- Parabens
- Phenylbenzimidazole (ensulizole)

NATURAL OILS WITH SPF

Did you know there are tons of nut, fruit and veggie oils that have naturally occurring SPF? Check it!

Oil	SPF
Red raspberry seed oil (protects against UVA and UVB rays)	30 to 50
Carrot seed essential oil	35 to 40
Wheat germ oil	20
Avocado oil	15
Hazelnut oil	15
Soybean oil	10
Coconut oil	8 to 10
Olive oil	8
Macadamia nut oil	6
Sweet almond oil	5
Jojoba oil	4
Rice bran oil	4

Chapter 5

Bath and Body Care

Basic Body Wash Base. 122

Invigorate-Me Body Wash 123

Zen Body Wash 124

Aphrodite Body Wash 126

Zit-Zapping Body Wash 127

Refreshing Footloose Soak 129

Orange Vanilla Bubble Bath . . . 130

Pick-Me-Up Bath Fizzy 132

Vanilla Cupcake Bath Salts. 135

Fruity and Floral Massage Oil . . .136

Oh My Sore Muscles! Oil 139

Awesome Aloe Vera
   Body Scrub. 140

Almond Sugar Body Scrub. 142

DIY Almond Milk. 143

Vanilla Latte Body Scrub 145

Coffee Body Scrub 146

Sea Salt Body Scrub 147

Holiday Pumpkin Pie
   Body Scrub. 148

Flaxseed Body Scrub 150

Sugar Cookie Body Scrub 151

Easy-Peasy Two-Ingredient
   Body Butter 152

Chocolate Orange Whipped
   Body Butter 154

Unicorn Kisses
   Shimmer Lotion. 156

Sparklepuss Glitter Gel. 158

Chamomile and Lavender
   Sleepytime Lotion 159

Heavenly Lotion Bars 160

Fall Pumpkin Deep-Moisturizing
   Body Treatment 163

Go-Go Jojoba Solid Perfume. . . 164

Take Me Away Essential Oil
   Perfume 166

Fruity and Floral Vanilla
   Perfume 167

Uniquely You Essential Oil
   Perfume 168

Preggo-Essential
   Stretch Mark–Prevention
   Cream 170

Bodacious Beer Beauty
   Recipes 171

Basic Body Wash Base

This recipe is the main component of all the luscious body washes in this book. It's a nice, unscented starting point you can build on. Once you've tried the recipes on pages 123 to 127, experiment! Add whatever essential oils you like to the base, depending on the feeling you want to experience, from relaxed to energized.

Best for:

♥ All skin types, including babies' skin

TOP TIP: Vegetable glycerin is a natural humectant made from plant seed oils that helps the skin draw and lock in moisture. When you're shopping for glycerin, make sure it's 100% plant-based (I'm not spreading any moo goo on this bod!). Plus, glycerin derived from petroleum or animal fat can actually zap moisture from your skin, and that's whack.

★ Superstar ingredient: Castile soap is a vegetable oil–based soap, traditionally made with olive oil. It has a bazillion uses, so I recommend stocking up. You can use it as a body wash, shampoo, makeup brush cleaner, laundry detergent, dish soap, hand soap or all-purpose cleaner. You name it, you can use castile soap on it.

- Bottle with lid

½ cup	unscented liquid castile soap	125 mL
¼ cup	liquid vegetable glycerin	60 mL
3 tbsp	sweet almond oil (see info, page 136)	45 mL

1. Pour castile soap, vegetable glycerin and sweet almond oil into bottle. Shake gently until combined.

2. Gently shake bottle to recombine before each use. Pour a small amount of body wash into palm or onto a damp washcloth, and massage all over skin in the shower, using circular motions.

3. Rinse skin with warm water and pat dry with a towel. Follow with your favorite body moisturizer.

4. Store in the shower for up to 6 months.

Find Your Bliss

Think of this chapter as a guide to creating your own perfect-for-you mini-spa. Whip up the products you're interested in, light a few candles, put on your favorite music and let it all go as you beautify yourself. You'll emerge relaxed and renewed in body *and* mind.

Invigorate-Me Body Wash

If you're feeling sluggish, this wash will kick you in the pants (in a good way, of course!). This trio of herb essential oils is a hella-good, all-natural wake-up call.

Best for:

♥ All skin types, especially 🌢 Oily/acne-prone

TOP TiP: Too short on time to make the Basic Body Wash Base? Substitute a scant 1 cup (250 mL) of unscented liquid castile soap for the base. It's a neutral, ready-to-use vegan soap you can dress up any way you like.

● *Bottle with lid*

1	batch Basic Body Wash Base (opposite)	1
20	drops lavender essential oil (see Superstar ingredient, page 124)	20
10	drops rosemary essential oil (see Caution, page 91)	10
10	drops peppermint essential oil	10

1. Pour Basic Body Wash Base, and lavender, rosemary and peppermint essential oils into bottle. Shake gently until well combined.

2. Gently shake bottle to recombine before each use. Pour a small amount of body wash into palm or onto a damp washcloth, and massage all over skin in the shower, using circular motions.

3. Rinse skin with warm water and pat dry with a towel. Follow with your favorite body moisturizer.

4. Store in the shower for up to 6 months.

DID YOU KNOW?

Studies have proven that peppermint can wake up snoozy drivers. Try popping peppermints in the car or opening a bottle of peppermint essential oil and taking about eight sniffs. Awake now? Good!

Zen Body Wash

Need to turn down the volume on your stress level and get your Zen on? This body wash brings out your inner peace with chill sandalwood and calm-inducing lavender and clary sage.

Best for:

♥ All skin types

TOP TIP: Too short on time to make the Basic Body Wash Base? Substitute a scant 1 cup (250 mL) of unscented liquid castile soap for the base. It's a neutral, ready-to-use vegan soap you can dress up any way you like.

★ Superstar ingredient: Lavender has been shown to decrease both your heart rate and blood pressure. This relaxes the body and primes you to get a better night's sleep.

- *Bottle with lid*
- *Small funnel*
- *Bottle with pump top*

1	batch Basic Body Wash Base (page 122)	1
25	drops sandalwood essential oil (see Did you know?, page 126)	25
10	drops lavender essential oil	10
5	drops clary sage essential oil (see Caution, page 182)	5

1. Pour Basic Body Wash Base, and sandalwood, lavender and clary sage essential oils into bottle. Shake gently until well combined. Using funnel, pour into pump-top bottle.

2. Gently shake bottle to recombine before each use. Pour a small amount of body wash into palm or onto a damp washcloth, and massage all over skin in the shower, using circular motions.

3. Rinse skin with warm water and pat dry with a towel. Follow with your favorite body moisturizer.

4. Store in the shower for up to 6 months.

Aphrodite Body Wash

It's time to get your sexy on! The earthy, floral aroma of this fantastic body wash is guaranteed to get you more in touch with your feminine side.

Best for:

♥ All skin types, especially ▲ Dry

★ Superstar ingredient:

Patchouli essential oil has an irresistible, earthy, naturally musky fragrance. It's extracted via steam distillation from the leaves of the patchouli plant (*Pogostemon cablin*). This essential oil can help improve the appearance of dry, dull skin.

- Bottle with lid

1	batch Basic Body Wash Base (page 122), see Top tip, opposite	1
10	drops lavender essential oil (see Superstar ingredient, page 124)	10
5	drops sandalwood essential oil	5
5	drops jasmine essential oil (see Caution, below)	5
5	drops sweet orange essential oil (see info, page 130)	5
5	drops patchouli essential oil	5
5	drops ylang-ylang essential oil	5

1. Pour Basic Body Wash Base, and lavender, sandalwood, jasmine, sweet orange, patchouli and ylang-ylang essential oils into bottle. Shake gently until well combined.

2. Gently shake bottle to recombine before each use. Pour a small amount of body wash into palm or onto a damp washcloth, and massage all over skin in the shower, using circular motions.

3. Rinse skin with warm water and pat dry with a towel. Follow with your favorite body moisturizer.

4. Store in the shower for up to 6 months.

Caution: Do not use jasmine essential oil if you are or might be pregnant.

DID YOU KNOW?
True sandalwood essential oil is distilled from the Indian sandalwood plant (Santalum album). It is always in demand as a fragrance and an ingredient in beauty products, so resources are scarce. The best way to conserve this species is to avoid using essential oil made from it (or use it sparingly). More-available substitutes are Australian sandalwood (Santalum spicatum), Hawaiian sandalwood (Santalum paniculatum) and Amyris (Amyris balsamifera, or West Indian sandalwood).

Zit-Zapping Body Wash

Zits suck. Period. Hormones, clogged pores and excess bacteria can all cause these pesky spots to rear their ugly heads, and not just on your face. This body wash will help you say buh-bye to body acne from head to toe.

Best for:

● Oily/acne-prone skin

TOP TIP: Too short on time to make the Basic Body Wash Base? Substitute a scant 1 cup (250 mL) of unscented liquid castile soap for the base. It's a neutral, ready-to-use vegan soap you can dress up any way you like.

● *Bottle with lid*

1	batch Basic Body Wash Base (page 122)	1
20	drops Roman chamomile essential oil	20
10	drops tea tree essential oil (see info, page 84)	10
10	drops lemon essential oil (see info, page 132)	10

1. Pour Basic Body Wash Base, and Roman chamomile, tea tree and lemon essential oils into bottle. Shake gently until well combined.

2. Gently shake bottle to recombine before each use. Pour a small amount of body wash into palm or onto a damp washcloth, and massage all over skin in the shower, using circular motions.

3. Rinse skin with warm water and pat dry with a towel. Follow with your favorite body moisturizer.

4. Store in the shower for up to 6 months.

Refreshing Footloose Soak

It's amazing how a little warm, mineral-laced water can work miracles on tired, achy feet. Soften and hydrate your hardworking tootsies with this simple soak while you catch up on some trashy celeb gossip magazines (guilty pleasure!) or binge-watch your fave Netflix show.

Best for:

♥ All skin types

TOP TIPS: Rosemary essential oil has antifungal superpowers. It has also been shown to fight bacteria, so it keeps feet smelling sweet.

If you like, add a pinch of dried rosemary and a sprig of fresh mint to your soak. It smells extra heavenly.

★ Superstar ingredients: Epsom salt chills out tired, aching feet, while baking soda helps eliminate and prevent foot odor. Peppermint and rosemary essential oils awaken the senses while they banish bad-smelling bacteria.

- *Glass jar with lid*
- *Basin or bucket large enough to accommodate feet comfortably*

1 cup	fine Epsom salt	250 mL
½ cup	baking soda	125 mL
15	drops peppermint essential oil	15
15	drops rosemary essential oil (see Caution, page 91)	15
	Hot water	

1. In a medium bowl, stir together Epsom salt, baking soda, peppermint essential oil and rosemary essential oil until well combined. Spoon into jar.

2. Fill basin with hot water. Add ¼ cup (60 mL) of the Epsom salt mixture and stir until dissolved. Let cool slightly.

3. Test the temperature of the water with your toe to make sure it's very warm but not scalding. Immerse your feet in the water and soak for 15 to 30 minutes (longer is OK, if you like).

4. Pat feet dry with a towel. Follow with your favorite moisturizing cream or straight-up coconut or jojoba oil.

5. Store jar at room temperature for up to 6 months.

DID YOU KNOW? Epsom salt is not the same as table salt (sodium chloride). It is the crystallized form of magnesium sulfate. Try adding it to warm bathwater to loosen sore muscles and soak your troubles away.

Orange Vanilla Bubble Bath

Vanilla and orange is one of my favorite scent combos. When those two get together, they create a yummy, mood-boosting aroma, like a vegan Creamsicle, that makes me smile. Turn off your phone, pour a bit of this potion into the tub, settle in and go to your happy place.

Best for:

♥ All skin types

TOP TiP: You'll usually see the botanical names of plants on bottles of essential oil. In this case, look for oil made from sweet oranges, or *Citrus sinensis*.

★ Superstar ingredient:

Orange essential oil is mega-useful because it's everything from aphrodisiac to antibacterial to antiseptic. It boosts immunity and your mood, keeping you healthy, happy and relaxed.

- *Funnel*
- *Glass bottle with lid*

1 cup	unscented liquid castile soap (see Superstar ingredient, page 122)	250 mL
½ cup	liquid vegetable glycerin (see Top tip, page 122)	125 mL
2 tbsp	vanilla powder (see info, page 151)	30 mL
2 tbsp	filtered water	30 mL
40	drops sweet orange essential oil	40

1. Using funnel, pour castile soap, vegetable glycerin, vanilla powder, water and orange essential oil into bottle. Shake gently until well combined.

2. Gently shake bottle to recombine before each use. Add ¼ cup (60 mL) of bubble bath to warm bathwater. Soak in bath for about 20 minutes.

3. Rinse skin with warm water and pat dry with a towel. Follow with your favorite body moisturizer.

4. Store at room temperature for up to 2 months.

DID YOU KNOW? Orange essential oil is made from orange peels through a process known as cold compression, which squeezes the oil out of the rind without using steam or solvents. It keeps the oil totally pure and ensures it smells amazing.

Pick-Me-Up Bath Fizzy

Looking for an energy boost? Mix up these heavenly bath bombs, drop one in the tub and let the fizzy magic commence. You'll instantly feel the energizing *zing* of the uplifting essential oils hard at work.

Best for:

♥ All skin types, especially ● Oily/ acne-prone

TOP TiPS: You can use lots of different kitchen items to make bath fizzies. Metal or silicone molds (in any shape) work really well, as do ice cube trays and muffin pans.

To make fizzies that look like the ones in the photos, add powdered or dried herbs, grated citrus zest and/or flowers to the dry ingredients. Just make sure the pieces are small. Add some more to the mold before scooping in the moistened mixture, if you like.

★ Superstar ingredient: Lemon
essential oil detoxifies skin and acts as an astringent, banishing blemishes on oily skin. It also brightens dull skin, making it dewy and fresh.

- *Spray bottle*
- *Small metal or silicone molds*

1 cup	baking soda	250 mL
½ cup	fine Epsom salt (see info, page 129)	125 mL
½ cup	citric acid powder	125 mL
1 tbsp	filtered water	15 mL
2 tsp	jojoba oil (see info, page 65)	10 mL
40	drops lemon essential oil	40
20	drops peppermint essential oil (see Did you know?, page 123)	20
	All-natural food coloring (optional)	

1. In a medium bowl, whisk together baking soda, Epsom salt and citric acid powder until well combined.

2. In bottle, shake together water, jojoba oil, lemon essential oil, peppermint essential oil and a few drops of food coloring (if using) until blended.

3. Spray jojoba oil mixture over baking soda mixture until barely moistened.

4. Scoop into metal molds, smoothing tops and pressing firmly to compress into cakes. Let stand at room temperature for 2 to 3 hours or until bath fizzies are firm and hold their shape.

5. Gently remove bath fizzies from molds. Transfer to an airtight container.

6. Drop 1 bath fizzy into warm bathwater. Soak in bath for about 20 minutes.

7. Rinse skin with warm water and pat dry with a towel. Follow with your favorite body moisturizer.

8. Store airtight container at room temperature for up to 2 months.

DID YOU KNOW?
The delicious scent of lemon essential oil keeps you alert and aware, and helps you overcome fatigue. In fact, Japanese researchers discovered that when it was diffused throughout a busy office, typing errors dropped by more than 50%!

Vanilla Cupcake Bath Salts

All right, all you cupcake lovers, these bath salts are guaranteed to woo your nostrils without breaking the bank — although they may tempt your sweet tooth. The recipe makes 1½ cups of bath salts, or enough for about three divine, relaxing, vanilla-scented soaks.

Best for:

♥ All skin types

★ Superstar ingredient:

Antioxidants in vanilla absolute promote healing. They also neutralize free radicals; these nasty buggers are released during regular cell metabolism and when you're exposed to environmental toxins, and they can damage your cells. Bonus: vanilla acts as an aphrodisiac, boosting the secretion of the hormones estrogen and testosterone. Rowr!

- Glass jar with lid

¾ cup	fine Epsom salt (see info, page 129)	175 mL
½ cup	Himalayan pink salt	125 mL
¼ cup	baking soda (see Did you know?, page 94)	60 mL
6 to 8	drops vanilla absolute	6 to 8
2 tbsp	dried herbs or flowers, or cupcake sprinkles (optional)	30 mL
	All-natural food coloring (optional)	

1. In a medium bowl, stir together Epsom salt, Himalayan pink salt, baking soda, vanilla absolute, herbs (if using) and a few drops of food coloring (if using) until well combined. Spoon into jar.

2. Add about ½ cup (125 mL) of bath salts to warm bathwater. Soak in bath for about 20 minutes.

3. Rinse skin with warm water and pat dry with a towel. Follow with your favorite body moisturizer.

4. Store at room temperature for up to 6 months.

DID YOU KNOW?
Vanilla absolute is made from fermented vanilla beans, which grow on a creeper plant, or vine, that's native to Mexico.

Fruity and Floral Massage Oil

This oil is fantastic whether you're on the giving or receiving end of a massage. The ingredients are relaxing, healing and moisturizing. Plus, they make this formula smell ah-mazing!

Best for:

♥ All skin types

TOP TiP: Massage therapy improves immunity, defuses stress, eases anxiety and depression, and reduces tension headaches and muscle pain. All the more reason to indulge in a massage with this luxurious oil.

★ Superstar ingredients:

Sweet almond oil is made by pressing sweet almonds, or the nuts we typically eat. (Bitter almonds are another species and make a different type of oil.) Sweet almond oil is super-rich in vitamin E (alpha-tocopherol) and essential fatty acids. When you boost almond oil's powers with a little vitamin E oil, you have a potent mixture that soothes, softens and heals dry, tired skin.

- Small funnel
- Glass bottle with lid

1 cup	sweet almond oil	250 mL
½ tsp	vitamin E oil	2 mL
40	drops lavender essential oil (see Superstar ingredient, page 124)	40
40	drops grapefruit essential oil	40

1. Using funnel, pour sweet almond oil, vitamin E oil, lavender essential oil and grapefruit essential oil into bottle. Shake vigorously until well combined.

2. Apply a small amount of oil to palms and rub to warm. Massage into skin, reapplying as necessary.

3. Store at room temperature for up to 6 months.

DID YOU KNOW?

Almond trees have been cultivated for more than 5,000 years. They grow best in hot, dry climates. The trees bloom and form fruity pods; in the very center of the pods are the almond kernels. They are harvested when the pods split open.

Oh My Sore Muscles! Oil

If you've overdone it or just started exercising, chances are you'll walk away with general achiness, and sore buns, abs and thighs. Hey, no pain, no gain, right? Just apply this mixture to ouchie spots and start to feel the pain melt away. Another round of tennis, anyone?

Best for:

Sore, aching muscles

TOP TIP: Clove bud essential oils are made from both the buds and the leaves of the clove plant. For this recipe, you want the pain-relieving oil from the buds.

★ Superstar ingredients:

Wintergreen essential oil is extracted from the plant's leaves and has a fresh, minty scent. It relieves both muscle and joint pain, and is used in aromatherapy; the aromatherapist diffuses it into the air to facilitate relaxation and improve mood. Like wintergreen oil, chamomile oil helps you see the glass as half full, easing feelings of sadness, disappointment and sluggishness. You can inhale the aromas from each of these oils directly from the bottle. Try eight to 10 deep inhalations when you're stressed.

- *Small glass bottle with roll-on top*

2 tbsp	coconut oil (see info, page 170)	30 mL
10	drops chamomile essential oil	10
3	drops wintergreen essential oil (see Caution, below)	3
3	drops lavender essential oil (see Superstar ingredient, page 124)	3
1	drop clove bud essential oil	1
	Flowers or herbs (optional)	

1. Place coconut oil in a small heatproof glass bowl. Microwave on High, stirring every 5 seconds, until melted and completely smooth. (The total time will depend on the strength of your microwave.)

2. Stir in chamomile, wintergreen, lavender and clove bud essential oils until well combined. Let stand until cool to the touch. Pour into bottle. Add flowers (if using).

3. Roll oil over sore muscles and massage.

DID YOU KNOW? Native Americans used wintergreen for centuries to treat respiratory tract infections and improve endurance when running.

Caution: Never ingest wintergreen or any other essential oil without talking to your doctor first. Do not use clove bud essential oil or wintergreen essential oil if you are or might be pregnant. Also, don't apply wintergreen essential oil directly to skin, as it can be an irritant. Use it sparingly and dilute it in a carrier oil, such as olive or coconut oil.

Awesome Aloe Vera Body Scrub

Here's an easy way to incorporate miraculous aloe vera into your beauty routine. This scrub leaves your skin über-nourished and youthful-looking. Customize it with your favorite essential oil. I love anything in the citrus family for this scrub.

Best for:

♥ All skin types, especially ▲ Dry and ⬤ Oily/acne-prone

TOP TIP: Grow your own aloe vera plant on a kitchen windowsill. Break off a leaf to reveal the clear gel you need for this recipe. You can also apply it directly to minor wounds and burns.

★ Superstar ingredient: Aloe vera really is a miracle plant. It is mega-moisturizing because it contains about 99% water, and the skin actually absorbs its liquid faster than it does water! Aloe vera is packed with vitamins, minerals, amino acids, enzymes and natural antiseptics. It also contains auxins and gibberellins, or hormones that have anti-inflammatory powers. They help speed up healing and reduce scarring.

- *Jar with lid*

1 cup	sea salt (see info, page 147)	250 mL
2 tbsp	aloe vera gel	30 mL
2 tbsp	coconut, jojoba, olive, sweet almond or grapeseed oil	30 mL
10 to 15	drops essential oil(s) of your choice	10 to 15

1. In a medium bowl, stir together sea salt, aloe vera gel, coconut oil and essential oil(s) until well combined. Spoon into jar.

2. Using hands, massage a small amount of scrub all over skin in the shower, using circular motions.

3. Rinse skin with warm water and pat dry with a towel. Follow with your favorite body moisturizer.

4. Store in the shower for up to 6 months.

DID YOU KNOW? The Ancient Egyptians called aloe vera the "plant of immortality." This medicinal plant looks like a cactus and loves dry climates, but it's actually a member of the lily family.

Almond Sugar Body Scrub

When I make DIY Almond Milk (opposite), I always have almond pulp left over. I don't like seeing it go to waste, so being my thrifty, beautylicious self, I transform it into skin-care products. This scrub is mega-simple to make, and it smells delish! It also kicks some serious ass at getting rid of icky dead skin cells, revealing soft, glowing skin underneath.

Best for:

♥ All skin types

TOP TiP: You can also use sweet almond oil to lighten up dark under-eye circles. Dab a few drops onto your skin, and gently massage until the oil is absorbed. Do this daily, and you'll see results within 2 weeks.

★ Superstar ingredient: Sweet almond oil is nutrient-rich and full of antioxidants, including skin-protecting vitamin E. This vitamin also acts as a preservative for the scrub, extending its shelf life. Sweet almond oil also contains essential fatty acids, which make skin smooth and supple, and protein, one of the basic building blocks of skin. The abundant magnesium in this oil protects against stress and aging, and it helps your body absorb calcium and other useful nutrients.

- Jar with lid

¼ cup	leftover almond pulp (see Top tips, opposite) or ground almonds	60 mL
¼ cup	packed vegan brown sugar (see Top tip, page 145)	60 mL
¼ cup	sweet almond oil	60 mL

1. In a small bowl, stir together almond pulp, brown sugar and sweet almond oil until well combined. Spoon into jar.

2. Using hands, massage a small amount of scrub all over skin in the shower, using circular motions.

3. Rinse skin with warm water and pat dry with a towel. Follow with your favorite body moisturizer.

4. Store in the shower for up to 6 months.

> **DID YOU KNOW?**
> The almonds here are ground with their skins on, so they have the ideal coarse texture for making a body scrub. Almond flour is more finely ground; it's made from blanched almonds, which don't have skins. It's too fine for a good scrub, so save it for making delicious vegan cakes.

DIY Almond Milk

Before, whenever I heard that people were making their own nut or grain milks, my gut reaction was, "Who has time for that?!" Turns out, we all do. Making milks from almonds (or cashews, soybeans, oats and so on) is super-easy. It saves cash, it's hella gratifying to make something so tasty from scratch *and* it makes leftovers you can use in homemade beauty products.

Best for:

Drinking, putting on cereal and adding to recipes

TOP TiPS: You can dress up your almond milk with vanilla extract or cinnamon, if you like. If you like it sweetened, add some ground dates, agave syrup, maple syrup or puréed banana. Have fun and experiment with different flavorings and natural vegan sweeteners.

Don't forget to save the leftover almond pulp to make Almond Sugar Body Scrub (opposite). You can also dehydrate the pulp to create almond flour for baking.

- *Blender*
- *Nylon mesh bag for straining*

8 cups	filtered water, divided	2 L
1 cup	raw almonds	250 mL
	Flavorings or sweeteners (optional)	

1. In a large bowl, combine 4 cups (1 L) of the water with almonds. Let stand for 12 to 24 hours.

2. Drain almonds and rinse under cold water. Drain well.

3. In blender, combine almonds with remaining 4 cups (1 L) water. Blend until smooth and milky colored.

4. Working over another large bowl, pour almond mixture into mesh bag. Squeeze bag to remove all of the liquid. Reserve pulp for another use.

5. Stir flavorings (if using) into almond milk. Return to blender. Blend until smooth and well combined.

6. Store in the refrigerator for up to 1 week.

DID YOU KNOW?
In the Victorian era, the almond blossom represented hope. It was common for women to pin sprigs of the blossoms onto their clothes.

Vanilla Latte Body Scrub

Coffee makes mornings way better, am I right? It's also naturally anti-inflammatory and rich in antioxidants, making it a perfect wake-up for your skin. This wicked scrub pairs the awesomeness of coffee with ultra-moisturizing coconut oil, and is super-simple to whip up from ingredients that are already in your kitchen.

Best for:

♥ All skin types

TOP TIP: Bone char is used to process many types of sugar, including granulated, brown and confectioner's (icing) sugars. Health food stores often have specially labeled vegan sugars you can buy. Beet sugar is usually a vegan-friendly option.

★ Superstar ingredient:

The caffeine in coffee is chock-full of antioxidants that squash nasty free radicals. This helps prevent signs of premature aging, including wrinkles, sun spots and fine lines. Caffeine also improves circulation in the skin and reduces swelling and inflammation.

• Large jar with lid

½ cup	coconut oil (see info, page 170)	125 mL
1 cup	freshly ground coffee or leftover coffee grounds	250 mL
1 cup	vegan granulated sugar	250 mL
2 tsp	vanilla powder (see info, page 151)	10 mL

1. In a small saucepan over low heat, melt coconut oil.

2. In a large bowl, stir together coconut oil, coffee, sugar and vanilla powder until well combined. Spoon into jar.

3. Using hands, massage a small amount of scrub all over skin in the shower, using circular motions.

4. Rinse skin with warm water and pat dry with a towel. Follow with your favorite body moisturizer.

5. Store in the shower for up to 2 months.

DID YOU KNOW? Coffee grounds are a fantastic exfoliant. Plus, the caffeine they contain actually helps tighten and tone your skin, and can even diminish the appearance of cellulite. (Cellulite, people!)

Coffee Body Scrub

Ugh — cellulite is a total beyotch. Instead of spending all of your hard-earned money on gimmicky treatments and dimple creams, make your own cellulite blaster that actually works. And by works, I mean this cream helps reduce the appearance of unwanted lumps and bumps. Trust me, you're gonna love it!

Best for:

Treating cellulite

TOP TIP: Olive oil contains vitamin E, polyphenols and phytosterols, all powerful antioxidants that help protect your skin from damage and aging. Vitamin E even protects against ultraviolet light.

★ **Superstar ingredient:** Coffee smells great, is rich in antioxidants and acts as an anti-inflammatory. The caffeine it contains, when combined with massage, firms and tightens the skin. (Massage also stimulates proper blood and lymph flow.) Meanwhile, olive, jojoba and coconut oil act as moisturizers, and brown sugar is a gentle exfoliant.

- Jar with lid

1 cup	freshly ground coffee or leftover coffee grounds	250 mL
6 tbsp	olive, jojoba or coconut oil	90 mL
3 tbsp	packed vegan brown sugar (see Top tip, page 145)	45 mL

1. In a medium bowl, stir together coffee, olive oil and brown sugar until well combined. Spoon into jar.

2. Using hands, massage a small amount of scrub all over skin in the shower, using circular motions.

3. Rinse skin with warm water and pat dry with a towel. Follow with your favorite body moisturizer.

4. Store in the shower for up to 6 months.

DID YOU KNOW? Cleopatra, the famous Egyptian Queen of the Nile, used olive oil to keep her skin naturally beautiful.

Sea Salt Body Scrub

Say hello to fresh-looking skin all over your bod. This simple scrub, powered by sea salt and scented with your favorite essential oils, will slough off dead, flaky skin and leave you looking (and feeling) younger.

Best for:

♥ All skin types

TOP TIP: Don't just add sea salt to this recipe; sprinkle it on your food, too. Sea salt contains 82 minerals and trace elements your body needs, including sodium, potassium, calcium, magnesium, chloride, iron, copper and zinc.

- Blender (optional)
- Jar with lid

1 cup	fine sea salt	250 mL
½ cup	grapeseed oil (see info, page 111)	125 mL
40	drops essential oil(s) of your choice	40

1. In blender, purée together sea salt, grapeseed oil and essential oil(s) until smooth. (Or in a small bowl, whisk ingredients together.) Spoon into jar.

2. Using hands, massage a small amount of scrub all over skin in the shower, using circular motions.

3. Rinse skin with warm water and pat dry with a towel. Follow with your favorite body moisturizer.

4. Store in the shower for up to 6 months.

DID YOU KNOW?

Sea salt is harvested in coastal areas and around saltwater lakes around the world. There are many famous companies that harvest sea salt in the Mediterranean Sea, the Atlantic Ocean and the North Sea. Unlike refined table salt, sea salt is minimally processed, so it is naturally moist and contains an array of minerals.

Holiday Pumpkin Pie Body Scrub

Fall is my favorite season because I can eat pumpkin pie and pumpkin soy nog like it's going out of style. In an effort to not OD on the edible stuff, I've created this recipe so you can enjoy it in a whole new way: on your skin. This yummy-smelling, exfoliating, pie-licious scrub also makes a great holiday gift.

Best for:

♥ All skin types

TOP TIP: Pure pumpkin isn't the same as pumpkin pie filling. It's just the 100% natural puréed cooked squash, with no added sugar, flavorings or other additives.

★ Superstar ingredient: Pumpkin

contains antioxidant vitamins A and C, which boost collagen production to keep your skin young. Pumpkin also contains alpha hydroxy acids (or AHAs, which are in lots of conventional acne treatments) and fruit enzymes, both of which increase cell turnover and renew the skin. This squash also contains essential fatty acids and vitamin E, another antioxidant that helps protect skin and regulate oil production. BTW, pumpkin is also high in zinc, which is good for fighting acne.

- *Jar with lid*

½ cup	canned pure pumpkin purée	125 mL
½ cup	packed vegan brown sugar (see Top tip, page 145)	125 mL
¼ tsp	ground cinnamon (see Did you know?, page 163)	1 mL

1. In a small bowl, stir together pumpkin purée, brown sugar and cinnamon until well combined. Spoon into jar.

2. Using hands, massage a small amount of scrub all over skin in the shower, using circular motions.

3. Rinse skin with warm water and pat dry with a towel. Follow with your favorite body moisturizer.

4. Cover and store any leftovers in the refrigerator for up to 2 weeks.

Flaxseed Body Scrub

Let's talk flax seeds: They. Are. Fab. The end. Seriously, they're packed with fatty acids, which increase your body's natural oil production, helping keep your skin youthful and soft. Flax seeds are also loaded with antioxidants (mega wrinkle fighters!), and they minimize inflammation. If you have acne, rosacea, dermatitis or psoriasis, you need this scrub.

Best for:

♥ All skin types, especially ● Oily/acne-prone, ▲ Dry and ◆ Sensitive

TOP TiP: You can grind fresh flax seeds or the leftover seeds from a batch of Flaxseed Hair-Styling Goop (page 194).

★ Superstar ingredient: The antioxidant and anti-inflammatory power of flax seeds (aka linseeds) comes from plant compounds called lignans. The seeds are rich in fiber, manganese, vitamin B_1 and alpha-linolenic acid (ALA), an omega-3 essential fatty acid. Research shows that consuming flax seeds can help lower your risk of developing diabetes, cancer and heart disease.

• *Blender (optional)*

2 tbsp	sweet almond, coconut, olive or jojoba oil	30 mL
1 tbsp	ground flax seeds	15 mL
2 tsp	vegan granulated sugar (see Top tip, page 145)	10 mL

1. In blender, purée together sweet almond oil, flax seeds and sugar until smooth. (Or in a small bowl, whisk ingredients together.)

2. Using hands, massage a small amount of scrub all over skin in the shower, using circular motions.

3. Rinse skin with warm water and pat dry with a towel. Follow with your favorite body moisturizer.

DID YOU KNOW?

Nutrient-rich flax seeds come from the flax plant, one of the most ancient fiber crops in the world; it is used to make linen. Flax was first cultivated in Babylon around 3000 BCE, and was grown in Ancient Egypt and China, as well. In fact, King Charlemagne, who ruled a large part of Western Europe in the eighth and ninth centuries, passed laws to ensure that his subjects ate these beneficial seeds.

Sugar Cookie Body Scrub

This scrub smells so scrumptious you won't know whether to eat it or rub it all over your body. It leaves skin glowing and moisturized, too.

Best for:

♥ All skin types

TOP TiP: Many processed foods are flavored with vanillin, a cheap artificial flavoring agent that has no nutritional or medicinal value.

★ Superstar ingredient:

Vanilla powder is made by grinding sun-dried whole vanilla beans. It offers up small amounts of vitamin C and calcium. It also gives foods a strong, pure vanilla flavor; try adding some to your next smoothie.

- Blender (optional)
- Jar with lid

¾ cup	vegan granulated sugar (see Top tip, page 145)	175 mL
½ cup	sweet almond oil (see info, page 136)	125 mL
2 tsp	vanilla powder	10 mL

1. In blender, purée together sugar, sweet almond oil and vanilla powder until smooth. (Or in a small bowl, whisk ingredients together.) Spoon into jar.

2. Using hands, massage a small amount of scrub all over skin in the shower, using circular motions.

3. Rinse skin with warm water and pat dry with a towel. Follow with your favorite body moisturizer.

4. Store in the shower for up to 6 months.

DID YOU KNOW?
Vanilla flowers are only pollinated naturally by bees in Mexico (and even there, only a few of these special insects survive). Elsewhere, the blossoms of this orchid have to be pollinated by hand, by humans.

Easy-Peasy Two-Ingredient Body Butter

This recipe is so simple, and so effective, you *have* to whip up a batch to put in your natural beauty kit. It's great on its own, but it's even better when you dress it up with a special essential oil blend that suits your mood.

Best for:

♥ All skin types

TOP TiP: If you don't have or want to use a hand mixer, throw the ingredients in a blender to whip them.

★ Superstar ingredient:

Skin just drinks up the moisture in coconut oil. This amazing, nutritious oil also contains anti-inflammatory antioxidants, and is antibacterial and antifungal, too.

- Hand mixer
- Large glass jar with lid

1 cup	cocoa butter, grated (see Top tips, page 84)	250 mL
1 cup	coconut oil	250 mL
	Essential oil(s) of your choice (optional), see box, opposite	

1. Place cocoa butter in a medium metal or heatproof glass bowl (see Top tips, page 84). Pour enough water into a medium saucepan to come about 1½ inches (4 cm) up the side; bring to a simmer. Place bowl on saucepan, making sure the bottom doesn't touch the water. Heat, stirring, for 5 to 10 minutes or until cocoa butter is melted and smooth.

2. Stir in coconut oil until melted. Remove bowl from heat. Refrigerate for 30 minutes until slightly firmer but still beatable.

3. Using hand mixer, beat at high speed for 10 minutes or until fluffy. Beat in essential oil blend (if using). Spoon into jar.

4. Using hands, massage a small amount of body butter all over body, concentrating on dry areas.

5. Store at room temperature for up to 6 months.

DID YOU KNOW?
Coconut oil is a great natural makeup remover. Try using it at night; it'll even wipe away waterproof mascara. Your face will love you!

MATCH YOUR MOOD

Easy-Peasy Two-Ingredient Body Butter (opposite) is the perfect backdrop for some awesome-smelling essential oil blends that increase your mental well-being. Just ask yourself: how do I want to feel today?

- **Focused:** 45 drops of peppermint essential oil (boosts mental clarity, improves concentration) + 40 drops of wild orange essential oil (cheerful, happy)

- **Uplifted:** 20 drops of lemon essential oil (refreshing, purifying) + 20 drops of wild orange essential oil (cheerful, happy) + 20 drops of lime essential oil (invigorating) + 20 drops of grapefruit essential oil (cooling, reviving)

- **Energized:** 60 drops of grapefruit essential oil (cooling, reviving) + 15 of drops peppermint essential oil (boosts mental clarity, improves concentration) + 10 drops of wintergreen essential oil (stimulating; see Caution, page 139)

- **Calm:** 50 drops of lavender essential oil (calming, relaxing) + 20 drops of vetiver essential oil (earthy, warm, calming) + 10 drops of sandalwood essential oil (boosts mental clarity, calming)

Chocolate Orange Whipped Body Butter

Smooth this body butter on, and your skin will drink in all the nutrients, making it refreshed, renewed and radiant. You'll glow with vibrant, healthy skin from head to toe. Bonus: you'll smell so scrumptious and sweet, your boo will wanna nibble on you!

Best for:

♥ All skin types

TOP TIP: Essential oils are super versatile. Inhale the aromas from a bottle of orange essential oil or add 8 to 10 drops to warm bathwater to detoxify your body and boost lymphatic and immune-system function. Or add the oil to a diffuser so you can enjoy its scent throughout your house.

- Hand mixer
- Glass jar with lid

¾ cup	coconut oil (see info, page 170)	175 mL
½ cup	cocoa butter, grated (see Top tips, page 84)	125 mL
1 tbsp	vitamin E oil (see Did you know?, page 214)	15 mL
1½ tsp	sweet almond oil (see info, page 136)	7 mL
50	drops sweet orange essential oil	50

1. In a medium metal or heatproof glass bowl, combine coconut oil and cocoa butter (see Top tips, page 84). Pour enough water into a medium saucepan to come about 1½ inches (4 cm) up the side; bring to a simmer. Place bowl on saucepan, making sure the bottom doesn't touch the water. Heat, stirring, for 5 to 10 minutes or until coconut oil mixture is melted and smooth.

2. Stir in vitamin E oil and sweet almond oil. Remove bowl from heat. Let cool to room temperature. Refrigerate for 30 minutes until slightly firmer but still beatable.

3. Using hand mixer, beat at high speed for 10 minutes or until fluffy, adding orange essential oil during the last minute. Spoon into jar.

4. Using hands, massage a small amount of body butter all over body, concentrating on dry areas.

5. Store at room temperature for up to 6 months.

DID YOU KNOW?
Orange essential oil has a balancing effect on the mind and body. It helps improve mood and reduces your stress level. Research shows that it can even help ease mild depression.

Unicorn Kisses Shimmer Lotion

If you want to let your inner magical unicorn shine through, you *need* to get your sparkle on. This super-simple lotion will help take your shimmer quotient to the next level. While this lotion is good for pretty much every skin type, it can be hard on some peeps with sensitive skin; if that's you, skip the essential oils or swap them out for soothing lavender or chamomile essential oil.

Best for:

♥ All skin types

TOP TIP: Mica is the name used to refer to minerals that grow in layers. They're crushed into a fine, translucent, shimmery powder that reflects the light. If you want a different-color glow, use silver, bronze or copper mica instead of gold.

★ Superstar ingredient: The aroma of lemon essential oil can eliminate mental fatigue, lower your anxiety level, and boost alertness and optimism. Open a bottle and inhale deeply 8 to 10 times to reset your mood, or add a few drops to an electric diffuser to fill the entire room with the oil's calming, wide-awake, citrusy scent.

• Glass jar with lid

1 cup	unscented Easy-Peasy Two-Ingredient Body Butter (page 152)	250 mL
1 tsp	gold mica powder	5 mL
40	drops orange essential oil (see info, page 130)	40
30	drops lemon essential oil	30
15	drops peppermint essential oil (see Did you know?, page 123)	15

1. In a medium bowl, whisk together Easy-Peasy Two-Ingredient Body Butter, mica powder, and orange, lemon and peppermint essential oils until well combined. Spoon into jar.

2. Using hands, massage a small amount of lotion over skin in areas where you'd like a glittery glow.

3. Store at room temperature for up to 6 months.

DID YOU KNOW?

Lemon essential oil is a natural astringent. It removes dead cells and brightens up dull skin. It also has antiseptic properties, so it's fab for treating pimples and controlling oily skin.

Sparklepuss Glitter Gel

Amp up your beauty game with this recipe. It will make you sparkle and stand out from the crowd on holidays, at parties or anywhere you need some extra glittery oomph. (Psst! This stuff will totally help nab the attention of that cute guy you spotted at the health food store. #yourewelcome.)

Best for:

♥ All skin types

★ Superstar ingredient: Aloe vera gel is the clear, jellylike pulp inside the leaves of the aloe vera plant. The gel is rich in glycoproteins and polysaccharides, which help reduce skin inflammation, ease pain and stimulate new cell growth. It's terrific at healing minor wounds.

• *Glass jar with lid*

1 cup	aloe vera gel	250 mL
	Gold mica powder (see Top tip, page 156)	

1. In a small bowl, stir aloe vera gel with enough of the mica powder to achieve the desired level of sparkle. Spoon into jar.

2. Using hands, massage a small amount of gel over skin in areas where you'd like a glittery glow.

3. Store at room temperature for up to 6 months.

DID YOU KNOW?
The Ancient Egyptians called aloe vera the "plant of immortality." This medicinal plant looks like a cactus and loves dry climates, but it's actually a member of the lily family.

Chamomile and Lavender Sleepytime Lotion

Add this recipe to your bedtime routine. First, draw a warm bath, and then add 8 to 10 drops of lavender (or another favorite relaxing) essential oil. Have a good soak, and after you towel off, apply this lotion all over your body. Sweet dreams!

Best for:

♥ All skin types

TOP TIP: Like lavender, Roman chamomile is a go-to cure for stress and anxiety. The essential oil made from this plant also helps ease feelings of grief, anger and emotional hypersensitivity.

★ Superstar ingredient:

Roman chamomile has anti-inflammatory properties, which help cool off red, inflamed skin caused by a number of conditions, including eczema. The essential oil also kills bacteria, fungi and viruses.

• Glass jar with lid

1 cup	unscented Easy Peasy Two-Ingredient Body Butter (page 152)	250 mL
10	drops lavender essential oil (see Superstar ingredient, page 124)	10
10	drops Roman chamomile essential oil	10

1. In a small bowl, whisk together Easy Peasy Two-Ingredient Body Butter, lavender essential oil and Roman chamomile essential oil. Spoon into jar.

2. Using hands, massage a small amount of lotion all over body.

3. Store at room temperature for up to 6 months.

DID YOU KNOW?
Roman chamomile is native to Northern Ireland and northwestern Europe. The flowers of Roman chamomile look like miniature daisies and smell a bit like apples.

eavenly Lotion Bars

DIY vegan lotion bars are my jam, and they should be yours, too. They are easy and inexpensive to whip up, completely natural and made with mega-nourishing ingredients. There are zero fillers, just skin-loving butters, oils and waxes. Plus, they're easy to travel with: just pop one in a tin and throw it in your bag.

Best for:

♥ All skin types

TOP TiP: Candelilla wax is the perfect vegan alternative to beeswax in creams, lotions and other beauty products. See box, below, for more on the amazing insects we call bees.

★ Superstar ingredient: Avocado oil deserves more press. It's loaded with nutrients, including antioxidant vitamins and minerals that your skin will love. The oil promotes the growth of collagen, which helps your skin stay firm, smooth and wrinkle-free (or at least wrinkle-minimized). It also helps skin retain moisture, keeping it smooth and supple, while soothing dryness and itching. Avocado oil is a natural treatment for skin conditions such as eczema and psoriasis, and it speeds up healing of wounds, burns and diaper rash.

- *Silicone molds or cupcake liners*

3 tbsp	candelilla wax	45 mL
3 tbsp	cocoa butter, grated (see Top tips, page 84)	45 mL
⅓ cup	avocado oil	75 mL
3 tbsp	shea butter (see Caution, page 220)	45 mL
60	drops essential oil(s) of your choice	60

1. In a small metal or heatproof glass bowl, combine candelilla wax and cocoa butter (see Top tips, page 84). Pour enough water into a small saucepan to come about 1½ inches (4 cm) up the side; bring to a simmer. Place bowl on saucepan, making sure the bottom doesn't touch the water. Heat, stirring, for 5 to 10 minutes or until candelilla wax mixture is melted and smooth.

2. Stir in avocado oil and shea butter until melted and smooth. Remove bowl from heat. Stir in essential oil(s) until well combined.

3. Pour into silicone molds. Let cool at room temperature for 1 hour or until solid. Turn over molds and release bars.

4. Rub a bar all over skin, focusing on dry areas.

5. Store in a cool, dark place or the refrigerator for up to 6 months.

The Bees' Knees

Honeybees are amazing, complex creatures. Tens of thousands of them coexist in each hive. They're ruled by a queen, who can live for as long as seven years, and each drone and worker bee has a distinct life mission to fulfill. Unfortunately, honeybees are being decimated by pesticides. For more information, visit www.peta.org and check out the honey industry fact sheet.

Fall Pumpkin Deep-Moisturizing Body Treatment

I wanted to share this delectable pumpkin body treat with y'all because it's seasonal and mad-yummy, and works wonders on dry skin. As soon as the temp begins to drop, I usually develop gnarly, scaly skin and turn into a dry, crusty ogre. But with this hydrator in hand, I'm soft and way lovelier.

Best for:

▲ Dry skin

★ **Superstar ingredient:** Pumpkin is naturally loaded with exfoliating enzymes and powerful nutrients that make your body glow. This includes vitamin C, which helps build collagen, and protects against wrinkle- and cancer-causing free radicals. Pumpkin also offers circulation-boosting B vitamins and UV damage–fighting carotenoids (plant-based antioxidant pigments that make pumpkin orange). These big squashes are also chock-full of minerals, including potassium, iron, copper and zinc, which all promote healthy skin.

- Glass jar with lid

½ cup	canned pure pumpkin purée (see Top tip, page 148)	125 mL
½ cup	coconut oil (see info, page 170)	125 mL
½ tsp	ground cinnamon	2 mL

1. In a small bowl, stir together pumpkin purée, coconut oil and cinnamon until very smooth. Spoon into jar.

2. Massage a small amount of mixture all over body, as you would a lotion. Let stand on skin for 10 to 15 minutes.

3. Rinse skin with warm water and pat dry with a towel.

4. Store in the refrigerator for up to 2 weeks.

DID YOU KNOW?
Cinnamon is naturally antimicrobial. It can help to banish acne and blemishes by drying up excess oil and improving circulation. It's also a natural exfoliant. Cinnamon on its own can burn a bit, so don't apply it directly to your skin; instead, enjoy its powers in mixtures like this.

o-Go Jojoba Solid Perfume

Did you know that tons of perfumes contain *nasty* animal ingredients, such as whale barf (ambergris) and animal gland juice (civet and castoreum)?! Apart from taming the gross factor, another benefit of making your own scents is that you can customize them to capture your *je ne sais quoi*. This recipe is ridiculously simple, and homemade perfumes make really thoughtful gifts, too.

Best for:

♥ All skin types

TOP TiP: With so many options for unique essential oil blends, you can cater your perfume to match your current mood or set a specific tone for the day. Two super-simple combos to try are peppermint and grapefruit, or lavender and orange.

★ Superstar ingredient:
Jojoba oil is hydrating and hypoallergenic. Plus, it kills bacteria, viruses and fungi. It also eases aches and pains, and reduces inflammation. Jojoba contains skin-healing vitamin E, and omega-6 and omega-9 essential fatty acids, which make skin incredibly happy.

• *Lip balm tin or tube*

2 tsp	candelilla wax	10 mL
2 tsp	jojoba oil	10 mL
40 to 50	drops essential oil(s) of your choice	40 to 50

1. Place candelilla wax in a small metal or heatproof glass bowl (see Top tips, page 84). Pour enough water into a small saucepan to come about 1½ inches (4 cm) up the side; bring to a simmer. Place bowl on saucepan, making sure the bottom doesn't touch the water. Heat, stirring, for 5 to 10 minutes or until wax is melted and smooth.

2. Add jojoba oil and stir for 1 to 2 minutes or until well combined. Stir in essential oil(s). Immediately pour into lip balm tin. Let cool until solid.

3. Rub perfume on pulse points, such as wrists or neck.

4. Store at room temperature for up to 1 year.

DID YOU KNOW?
Candelilla wax is made from the natural coating on the stems of the shrub *Euphorbia cerifera*, which is native to Mexico and the southwestern United States. The wax coating on the stems keeps the plant hydrated during hot, dry weather. It works on your skin in much the same way, locking in moisture.

Take Me Away Essential Oil Perfume

With this recipe, you can create a customized oil-based scent that's all about you. It can make you remember people or places you love, or just smell so pretty it makes you feel fabulous. Either way, it's all good.

Best for:

♥ All skin types

TOP TIP: This recipe will work with just about any carrier oil you like. Feel free to experiment.

- *Small glass spray bottle*

2 tbsp	jojoba, grapeseed or sweet almond oil	30 mL
60 to 75	drops essential oil(s) of your choice (see box, below)	60 to 75

1. Pour jojoba oil and essential oil(s) into bottle. Shake vigorously to combine.

2. Gently shake bottle to recombine before each use.

3. Spray perfume on pulse points, such as wrists or neck.

4. Store at room temperature for up to 6 months.

Two Scents to Try

These are two of my favorite homemade oil perfumes. Once you've mastered these, get your thinking cap on and find a combo that suits your personality perfectly:

- **Woodland Mystic:** 45 drops of cedarwood essential oil + 15 drops of juniper berry essential oil + 5 drops of ylang-ylang essential oil. Do not use cedarwood or juniper berry essential oil if you are or might be pregnant.

- **Cupcake in a Bottle:** 35 drops of vanilla absolute (or pure vanilla extract) + 20 drops of cocoa essential oil (or fewer drops of cocoa absolute; let your nose be your guide) + 5 drops of ylang-ylang essential oil

DID YOU KNOW? Our senses of smell and our memories go hand-in-hand. We naturally gravitate toward scents that remind us of people and places we like, and aromas that make us feel good.

Fruity and Floral Vanilla Perfume

When it comes to wearing perfume, I can never decide between sweet and floral, so I decided to incorporate both of my faves in one scrumdiddlyumptious recipe. Apply this flowery, aromatic perfume and you'll cause a buzz.

Best for:

♥ All skin types

TOP TiP: Use bergamot essential oil to help ease sadness and mild depression. It lifts your mood by boosting blood flow in the body. The flavonoids in bergamot oil are also linked to increased activity of two happiness-inducing neurotransmitters: dopamine and serotonin. That reduces anxiety and tension, which helps you relax.

• Dark glass spray bottle

¼ cup	pure vanilla extract	60 mL
1 tsp	witch hazel (see Superstar ingredient, page 242)	5 mL
1 tsp	liquid vegetable glycerin (see Top tip, page 122)	5 mL
6	drops lavender essential oil (see Superstar ingredient, page 124)	6
5	drops lemon essential oil (see info, page 132)	5
5	drops bergamot essential oil (see Cautions, page 55)	5

1. Pour vanilla extract, witch hazel, vegetable glycerin, and lavender, lemon and bergamot essential oils into bottle. Shake vigorously to combine.

2. Gently shake bottle to recombine before each use.

3. Spray perfume on pulse points, such as wrists or neck.

4. Store at room temperature in a cool, dark place for up to 6 months.

DID YOU KNOW? Bergamot is a citrus fruit, and the essential oil is extracted from the rind. Earl Grey tea gets its citrus accent from bergamot essential oil.

Uniquely You Essential Oil Perfume

There's nothing quite like making a custom scent. You get to save some cha-ching and have the satisfaction of whipping up a batch of awesome — like a wizard!

Best for:

♥ All skin types

TOP TIP: Look for a pretty perfume bottle to store your homemade scent in. Homemade perfume makes a gorgeous gift.

- *Small glass bottle with roll-on top*

1 tbsp	jojoba or sweet almond oil	15 mL
1 tbsp	high-proof grain alcohol (such as vodka)	15 mL
	Essential oil blend (see box, below)	
2 tbsp	filtered water	30 mL

1. In a small bowl, stir together jojoba oil, alcohol and essential oil blend. Pour into bottle. Let stand for 48 hours (or longer if you prefer a stronger scent).

2. Add water and shake well to recombine. Gently shake bottle to recombine before each use.

3. Roll perfume over pulse points, such as wrists or neck.

4. Store at room temperature for up to 6 months.

Scents to Start With

You can scent your homemade perfume with just about any essential oil you like. Here are a few of my favorite blends to get your creative juices flowing:

- **Earthy & peaceful:** 50 drops of sweet orange essential oil + 10 drops of cedarwood essential oil + 10 drops of rosemary essential oil. Do not use cedarwood or rosemary essential oil if you are or might be pregnant.

- **Sexy & feminine:** 30 drops of bergamot essential oil + 25 drops of jasmine essential oil + 20 drops of sandalwood essential oil + 5 drops of rose essential oil. Do not use bergamot, jasmine or rose essential oil if you are or might be pregnant.

- **Floral & romantic:** 40 drops of palmarosa essential oil + 20 drops of rosewood essential oil + 10 drops of rose geranium essential oil + 10 drops of ylang-ylang essential oil

- **Young & flirty:** 70 drops of grapefruit essential oil + 10 drops of rose geranium essential oil + 10 drops of ylang-ylang essential oil

Preggo-Essential Stretch Mark–Prevention Cream

When I had buns 1 and 2 in the oven, I most definitely had stretch-mark prevention on the brain. Pregnancy aside, stretch marks can also result from weight gain and loss, so this is not an exclusively bun-in-the-oven recipe. If you're not prone to stretch marks (thank your mama for those delicious genes), use this recipe as a no-nonsense, nourishing after-bath moisturizer.

Best for:

♥ All skin types

TOP TIP: If you're preggers and can't reach, grab your sig other or BFF and have them rub you down with this soothing cream. Or just give yourself a gentle belly rub with it whenever the urge strikes.

★ **Superstar ingredient:** Coconut oil, when consumed regularly, gives skin an even tone and reduces the size of pores. It also boosts immunity and energy levels. Coconut oil contains important fatty acids (capric, carprylic and lauric acids) that have disinfectant and antimicrobial properties. These protect your skin from infection. Coconut also contains a small amount of antioxidant vitamin E, which helps protect the skin from free radical damage.

- Hand mixer
- Small glass jar with lid

2 tbsp	coconut oil	30 mL
2 tbsp	shea butter (see Caution, page 220) or cocoa butter, grated (see Top tips, page 84)	30 mL
1 tbsp	vitamin E oil (see Did you know?, page 214)	15 mL
4	drops lavender essential oil (see Superstar ingredient, page 124)	4

1. In a small metal or heatproof glass bowl, combine coconut oil and shea butter (see Top tips, page 84). Pour enough water into a small saucepan to come about 1½ inches (4 cm) up the side; bring to a simmer. Place bowl on saucepan, making sure the bottom doesn't touch the water. Heat, stirring, for 5 to 10 minutes or until coconut oil mixture is melted and smooth.

2. Remove bowl from heat. Stir in vitamin E oil and lavender essential oil until well combined.

3. Using hand mixer, beat at high speed for about 5 minutes or until creamy. Spoon into jar.

4. Using hands, massage a small amount of cream over areas prone to stretch marks, such as the thighs, buttocks and abdomen.

5. Store at room temperature for up to 6 months.

DID YOU KNOW?

Coconut oil contains saturated fats made up of medium-chain fatty acids (aka triglycerides). These fats have received a lot of bad press, but the ones in coconut oil are good for your health, and they keep your skin moist and smooth.

BEER IS BODACIOUS FOR BEAUTY

Did you know beer works wonders on skin and hair? It's loaded with bacteria-fighting antioxidants that can help clear up your complexion, and wonderful yeasty goodness that will give you mega-shiny hair. Plus, it just smells yummy, doesn't it? Try some of these simple DIY beer beauty treatments, and you'll be tipsy on how good you look. Cheers!

- **Fruity Beer Face Scrub.** Acne be gone! Mash 2 or 3 strawberries with a few drops of beer to make a paste. Rub the paste on your face, using circular motions. Let it stand on your skin for 15 to 20 minutes. Rinse with warm water and follow with your favorite toner and moisturizer.

- **Beer Bubble Bath.** Ready for a super-skin-softening soak in your favorite ale? Do it up! Simply mix unscented liquid castile soap with your favorite beer. Then, add it to the tub while you're running your bathwater. Use as little or as much as you like!

- **Beer Shampoo.** Add body and shine to your luscious locks by combining equal parts of your favorite beer and your favorite cruelty-free shampoo. Simply use it like normal shampoo and enjoy the glossy results.

- **Beer Conditioner.** Combine 1 cup (250 mL) of warm, flat beer and 1 tsp (5 mL) of jojoba or flaxseed oil. Mix everything together well (if you wanna get über-fancy, throw in some mashed avocado, too). Shampoo as usual and follow up with your DIY beer conditioner. Leave it on your hair for 5 to 10 minutes before rinsing. Dig your new volume and shine.

Not All Beer Is Vegan

Gasp! Did you have any idea? Some beers are filtered through products derived from animals, such as isinglass (better known as dried fish air bladders) and gelatin (the collagen that's created by boiling down animal parts, such as bones and sinews). Barf nation! Barnivore (www. barnivore.com) is a super-handy online directory of vegan and vegetarian beer, wine and liquor that will help you find the good stuff and rest easy. Bookmark that site!

Chapter 6

Hair Care

Peppermint Pow! Stimulating Shampoo .174

For Flakes' Sake Dandruff Shampoo. 176

Tea Tree Oil Leave-In Conditioner. 177

Lovely Lavender and Sage Conditioner .178

Cider Vinegar Hair Rehab Rinse. 180

Clarifying Lemon Rinse 181

Crystal-Clear Rinse for Brunettes. 182

Tangle Wrangler. 185

Deep Hydration Avocado Hair Mask 186

Cedarwood Essential Oil Hair-Growth Treatment 188

Rosemary Mint Anti-Frizz Serum 189

Lavender Luster Serum 191

Lavender Mint No-Poo. 192

Flaxseed Hair-Styling Goop 194

Beach Bunny Sea Salt Spray. 196

Hair Spray-bilizer 197

Peppermint Pow! Stimulating Shampoo

Y'all ready to wake up those lackluster locks from follicles to ends, all while boosting your mood and getting some tingly action on? Mmm-hmm, that's what I thought. Let's stimulate and energize that sexy hair and scalp of yours with this simple and gentle cleanser.

Best for:

♥ All hair types, especially ▲ Dry

TOP TiPS: Peppermint essential oil is nourishing for dry hair. Plus, it promotes hair growth by stimulating circulation.

Bonus: this recipe makes a terrific, smooth shaving cream, too.

• *Large bottle with pump top*

1 cup	filtered water	250 mL
1 cup	unscented liquid castile soap (see Superstar ingredient, page 122)	250 mL
2 tbsp	aloe vera gel (see info, page 140)	30 mL
2 tsp	jojoba oil (see info, page 65)	10 mL
60	drops peppermint essential oil	60
20	drops lavender essential oil (see info, page 178)	20

1. Pour water, castile soap, aloe vera gel, jojoba oil, peppermint essential oil and lavender essential oil into bottle. Shake vigorously until well combined.

2. Shake bottle to recombine before each use. Apply a small amount of shampoo directly to scalp. Using fingers, massage into lather.

3. Rinse hair with warm water. Follow with your favorite conditioner.

4. Store in the shower for up to 3 months.

Why DIY Hair Care Is the Bomb

Limp locks, lackluster strands, frizzies and flyaways — do I have the fixes for you! The formulas in this chapter ditch the harsh sulfates, silicones, parabens, fragrances and synthetic gunk in commercial products in favor of nutrient-dense, all-natural ingredients you'll find in your kitchen.

One heads-up before we begin: when you switch to an all-natural hair-care regimen, you'll need a bit of time for your hair to detox and reboot. I recommend starting this transition with a Clarifying Lemon Rinse (page 181). Then, whip up the DIY shampoos and conditioners that are right for your hair, and give your mane a couple of weeks to adapt to the new routine. In due time, your hair will purge the ickies and welcome the yummies. There might be some funky transition time in between, but hang in there. The results are soooooooooo worth it.

For Flakes' Sake Dandruff Shampoo

There's no sexy way to say it: dandruff is caused when your scalp sheds globs of dead skin cells. Yuck. Luckily, tea tree essential oil is a powerful and natural antifungal, antiseptic and antibacterial ingredient. It rocks at ridding your scalp of dandruff, and it smells fresh and clean.

Best for:

❋ Dandruff-prone hair

★ **Superstar ingredient:** Tea tree oil is an essential when it comes to keeping your scalp healthy and your hair shiny. The antifungal, antibacterial, antiseptic and anti-inflammatory compounds it contains sweep away nasty dandruff flakes and soothe itchy, dry skin on your scalp.

• *Large bottle with pump top*

1 cup	coconut milk	250 mL
1 cup	unscented liquid castile soap (see Superstar ingredient, page 122)	250 mL
2 tbsp	aloe vera gel (see info, page 140)	30 mL
2 tsp	avocado oil (see Superstar ingredient, page 191)	10 mL
¼ tsp	vitamin E oil (see Did you know?, page 214)	1 mL
50	drops tea tree essential oil	50
20	drops lavender essential oil (see info, page 178)	20

1. Pour coconut milk, castile soap, aloe vera gel, avocado oil, vitamin E oil, tea tree essential oil and lavender essential oil into bottle. Shake vigorously until well combined.

2. Shake bottle to recombine before each use. Apply a small amount of shampoo directly to scalp. Using fingers, massage into lather.

3. Rinse hair with warm water. Follow with your favorite dandruff-fighting conditioner.

4. Store in the shower for up to 2 weeks.

DID YOU KNOW?

Hair is made of a tough protein known as keratin. Each hair grows out of a follicle, with the hair bulb at its base, that's embedded in the skin on your scalp. Inside the hair bulb, blood vessels bring in nourishment, allowing cells to divide and grow. This builds the hair shaft and helps push it out so it's visible above the surface of the scalp. Genes determine how long your hair grows and its structure.

Tea Tree Oil Leave-In Conditioner

Leave-in conditioners are designed to moisturize, protect, de-frizz, strengthen and smooth your beloved hairsies. Unfortunately, many mainstream, store-bought versions contain chemicals, synthetic ingredients and silicone, which isn't water soluble; that means you can't wash it out. Here's a pure, effective and affordable alternative that won't stick to your hair like glue.

Best for:

♥ All hair types

TOP TiP: Try a tea tree essential oil scalp massage when you use this conditioner. Dilute 3 to 5 drops in 1 tsp (5 mL) of your favorite carrier oil (see pages 41 and 44). It will stimulate blood flow, nix inflammation and remove dead skin cells to improve hair growth. Plus, it feels really good.

★ **Superstar ingredient:** Aloe vera juice is alkaline, so it balances the pH level of the hair, which helps it grow. Healthy growth is also encouraged by the proteolytic enzymes in aloe, which sweep away dead skin cells and unplug hair follicles. Aloe vera also mega-moisturizes dry, damaged hair; soothes an itchy scalp; and prevents dandruff, while adding shine and controlling frizz. It even relieves symptoms of some uncomfortable scalp conditions, including seborrheic dermatitis and psoriasis.

• *Large glass spray bottle*

1 cup	filtered water	250 mL
½ cup	aloe vera juice	125 mL
½ cup	liquid vegetable glycerin (see Top tip, page 122)	125 mL
1 tbsp	jojoba oil (see info, page 65)	15 mL
1 tsp	vitamin E oil (see Did you know?, page 214)	5 mL
40	drops tea tree essential oil	40

1. Pour water, aloe vera juice, vegetable glycerin, jojoba oil, vitamin E oil and tea tree essential oil into bottle. Shake vigorously to combine.

2. Shake bottle to recombine before each use. Spray conditioner over damp hair after shampooing and conditioning. Comb through and leave in. Dry and style hair as usual.

3. Store in the refrigerator for up to 2 months.

Lovely Lavender and Sage Conditioner

Apply this clean-smelling, relaxing concoction to naturally nourish your hair and tame stress at the same time. It's the perfect twofer.

Best for:

♥ All hair types, especially ▲ Dry and ✳ Dandruff-prone

TOP TIP: Guar gum is a natural, gluten-free thickener made from guar beans. Look for this cream-colored powder in the natural baking ingredients section of the supermarket.

★ Superstar ingredients:

Lavender essential oil is terrific for everyone because it promotes hair growth, and treats itchiness and dandruff. This oil, extracted from the flowers, is a soothing tonic for jangled nerves and anxiety, and can help you go to sleep more easily. Just put a few drops on your pillowcase before bed and have sweet dreams. Clary sage essential oil is antiseptic and regulates sebum, so it's a fab natural hair tonic. It removes buildup on the scalp and can ease the symptoms of many different problems, including psoriasis.

- *Blender*
- *Jar with lid*

1¼ tsp	guar gum	6 mL
¾ tsp	jojoba oil (see info, page 65)	3 mL
1 cup	coconut milk	250 mL
20	drops lavender essential oil	20
10	drops clary sage essential oil (see Caution, page 182)	10

1. In blender, combine guar gum and jojoba oil. Blend at high speed until smooth.

2. Add coconut milk, lavender essential oil and clary sage essential oil and blend until well combined. Pour into jar.

3. Shake jar to recombine before each use. Apply a small amount of conditioner to washed hair and, using fingers or a comb, work through to ends. Let stand on hair for about 5 minutes.

4. Rinse hair with warm water. Dry and style hair as usual.

5. Store in the shower for up to 1 month.

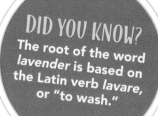

DID YOU KNOW? The root of the word lavender is based on the Latin verb *lavare,* or "to wash."

Cider Vinegar Hair Rehab Rinse

Cider vinegar is a rock-star DIY beauty ingredient. It contains alpha hydroxy acids and acetic acid, which increase blood flow to the scalp, balance hair and scalp pH, and clean up bacteria and product buildup. Cider vinegar brings hair back to life, leaving it soft, shiny and tangle-free.

Best for:

♥ All hair types

TOP TIP: When you make the tea for this recipe, save the damp tea bags. Place them on your eyelids and relax; this will reduce puffiness and dark under-eye circles. Put the tea bags in the fridge for even more anti-inflammatory cooling power.

★ **Superstar ingredient:** Green tea contains caffeine, which is stimulating to the skin. Green tea is also full of nourishing nutrients that boost overall wellness and improve hair health. Drinking green tea has been linked to lower blood pressure, cholesterol and triglyceride levels, and it can reduce your risk of developing type 2 diabetes, heart disease, stroke and cancer. Time to brew a cup? I think so!

● *Large spray bottle*

2 cups	cooled brewed green tea	500 mL
½ cup	cider vinegar (see info, page 185)	125 mL
5	drops clary sage or lavender essential oil (see Caution, page 182)	5

1. Pour green tea, cider vinegar and clary sage essential oil into bottle. Shake vigorously until well combined.

2. Shake bottle to recombine before each use. Spray rinse onto damp hair after shampooing and rinsing, using fingers to work through to ends. Let stand on hair for 2 to 3 minutes.

3. Rinse hair with warm water. Follow with your favorite conditioner.

4. Store in the shower for up to 2 weeks.

Variations

Cider Vinegar Hair Rehab Rinse for Dry Hair
Substitute myrrh or peppermint essential oil for the clary sage essential oil. Do not use myrrh essential oil if you are or might be pregnant.

Cider Vinegar Hair Rehab Rinse for Oily Hair
Substitute lemon, lemongrass or tea tree essential oil for the clary sage essential oil.

Cider Vinegar Hair Rehab Rinse for Dandruff-Prone Hair
Substitute eucalyptus essential oil for the clary sage essential oil.

DID YOU KNOW?
Green tea is the dried or steamed leaves of the Camellia sinensis plant, which is native to China. Black tea comes from the same plant; its leaves are oxidized, which increases the levels of caffeine and tannins.

Clarifying Lemon Rinse

Use this refreshing lemon rinse to sweep away product buildup and revive weighed-down strands. On light hair, it can also add pretty golden highlights. The rinse is also hella-good at treating dry scalp and dandruff.

Best for:

♥ All hair types, especially ▲ Dry and ❋ Dandruff-prone

TOP TiP: Lemon juice is a natural hair lightener. The best way to use it is to spend a day in the sun — wearing the sunscreen you whipped up on page 118, of course. The heat opens the hair cuticle, allowing the lemon juice to lift the color. Just squeeze a few fresh organic lemons, and add the juice to a spray bottle along with 1 tsp (5 mL) of coconut, jojoba or avocado oil to keep hair moisturized. Spray on and let the sun work its magic.

• Bottle with lid

1 cup	distilled water	250 mL
1 tsp	freshly squeezed lemon juice	5 mL

1. Pour water and lemon juice into bottle. Shake vigorously until well combined.

2. Shake bottle to recombine before each use. Pour rinse over damp scalp after shampooing and rinsing, using fingers to work through to ends. Let stand on hair for a few minutes.

3. Rinse hair with warm water. Follow with your favorite conditioner.

4. Store in the shower for up to 2 weeks.

Crystal-Clear Rinse for Brunettes

Dark-haired beauties, this rinse is for you. Just pour it on, rinse it out and get your chestnut shine on.

Best for:

♥ All hair types

TOP TIP: Studies have shown that the caffeine in black tea can block dihydrotestosterone (DHT), a hormone that causes hair loss. Black tea also makes hair soft, shiny and darker (covering up gray hair gradually and naturally). It also brings out your natural highlights. For an even easier treatment than this one, steep 2 to 4 black tea bags in 2 cups (500 mL) of boiling water overnight and use as a hair rinse.

★ Superstar ingredient: Sage comes from the leaves of the evergreen shrub *Salvia officinalis*, which is native to southern Europe near the Mediterranean Sea. Sage, a member of the mint family, naturally makes your hair soft and shiny, and invigorates your scalp, too.

Caution: Don't use sage or clary sage in any form if you are pregnant or nursing, or have epilepsy.

- Glass jar with lid
- Fine-mesh sieve
- Funnel
- Large bottle with lid

1 cup	cider vinegar (see info, page 185)	250 mL
3	black tea bags	3
1	small handful dried sage leaves (see Caution, below)	1
2 cups	filtered water	500 mL

1. In jar, combine cider vinegar, tea bags and sage leaves. Let stand in a warm place for 3 to 4 weeks, shaking mixture daily.

2. Pour vinegar mixture into a small saucepan and bring to a boil. Remove from heat. Let stand for 1 hour.

3. Place fine-mesh sieve over a large bowl. Strain liquid into bowl and discard solids. Stir in water. Using funnel, pour into bottle.

4. Pour rinse over damp hair after shampooing and rinsing, using fingers to work through to ends.

5. Rinse hair with warm water. Follow with your favorite conditioner.

6. Store in the refrigerator for up to 2 months.

DID YOU KNOW?

Sage gets its botanical name from the Latin word *salvare*, meaning "to heal or to save." The Ancient Romans and Greeks both prized sage and considered it to be a sacred plant. Ancient peoples also used it as a cure for baldness.

Tangle Wrangler

Does your hair get knotty and totally bug out? If so, I feel you! Tangled hair can be the worst. Leave it to good old cider vinegar (my BFF) to make it all better. Just spray this mixture on, comb it through and enjoy gorgeously smooth tresses.

Best for:

♥ All hair types, especially ▲ Dry

TOP TIPS: The acid in vinegar closes the cuticle of the hair, which helps it reflect light and appear shiny. When you're buying cider vinegar for DIY beauty recipes, choose one that's organic, raw, unfiltered and all-natural. It will be loaded with enzymes, minerals and nutrients.

If you have hard water, you may need to add a splash more cider vinegar to your formula. Hard water is alkaline and neutralizes the acidity of this spray.

• Glass spray bottle

1 cup	distilled or filtered water	250 mL
1 tbsp	cider vinegar	15 mL
20	drops lavender essential oil (see info, page 178)	20

1. Pour water, cider vinegar and lavender essential oil into bottle. Shake vigorously to combine.

2. Shake bottle to recombine before each use. Spray mixture over damp hair after shampooing and conditioning. Comb through and leave in. Dry and style hair as usual.

3. Store in the refrigerator for up to 2 months.

DID YOU KNOW?
Detanglers work by changing the surface texture of your hair. They smooth down the scales that line the outside of the strand. (Think of a crocodile's scales and you'll get the idea.) Many commercial detanglers prevent knots and static by coating hair with chemicals, such as oils or polymers. Cider vinegar has none of that yucky stuff, and it leaves zero greasiness behind.

Deep Hydration Avocado Hair Mask

If you've got truly unruly hair, this mask is going to be your new bestie. It quenches the thirst of parched hair and pampers strands that have been damaged by blow dryers, curling irons and chemicals. Best of all, it's edible — seriously! Spread any leftovers on toast with a sprinkle of salt, or plop them on vegan nachos.

Best for:

♥ All hair types, especially ▲ Dry

★ **Superstar ingredient:** Avocados soothe and soften hair and skin when you apply them externally. And when you eat them, you get lots of heart-healthy monounsaturated fats. They're also packed with fiber and a slew of vitamins and minerals, including potassium (they contain twice as much as bananas), folic acid, B vitamins and vitamin E. Avocados also boost the absorption of other nutrients, such as the fat-soluble vitamins A, D, E and K. Avocados are also high in vision-protecting lutein and osteoporosis-preventing calcium.

• *Blender*

1	ripe avocado	1
2 tbsp	olive oil	30 mL

1. Cut avocado in half and remove the pit. Cube and scoop out the flesh. Discard peel.

2. In blender, purée avocado with olive oil until smooth and creamy. Spoon into small bowl.

3. Apply mask to damp unwashed hair, using fingers or a comb to work through to ends. Let stand on hair for up to 1 hour.

4. Shampoo hair and rinse with warm water. Follow with your favorite conditioner.

DID YOU KNOW?
An avocado is actually a fruit, not a vegetable. It also goes by the names alligator pear or butter fruit.

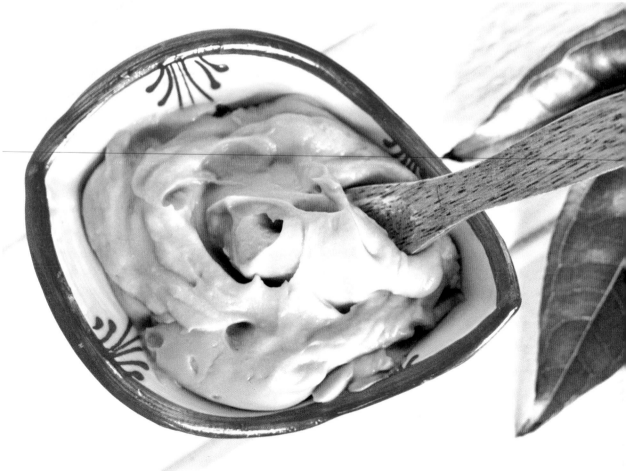

Cedarwood Essential Oil Hair-Growth Treatment

This simple recipe is a winner. It helps you grow your locks faster, prevents hair loss, treats split ends and dandruff, and keeps your hair mega-shiny.

Best for:

✳ Dandruff-prone,
▲ Dry and ≋ Thinning/brittle hair

TOP TIPS: Fellas, you can use this mixture as a sexy-smelling, nourishing beard oil, too.

Look for organic, cold-pressed 100% pure virgin castor oil in health food stores and online.

★ **Superstar ingredient:** Castor oil contains ricinoleic acid (an omega-9 fatty acid), which moisturizes the scalp, strengthens the roots of the hair and increases blood circulation, all of which improve hair growth. Castor oil also balances the pH of the scalp and helps preserve the scalp's natural oil balance. It nourishes hair with antioxidants, making it smoother, stronger, less frizzy and less prone to flyaways. The oil is also antibacterial, antifungal and antiviral, so it's an über-fab remedy for an itchy scalp and dandruff.

2 tbsp	castor oil	30 mL
5	drops cedarwood essential oil (See Caution, below)	5

1. In a small bowl, stir castor oil with cedarwood essential oil until well combined.

2. Massage treatment onto scalp before shampooing, using circular motions. Let stand on scalp for 30 minutes.

3. Shampoo hair and rinse with warm water. Follow with your favorite conditioner.

DID YOU KNOW?

Cedarwood essential oil is steam-distilled from the wood of the Virginia cedar tree, or *Juniperus virginiana*. It promotes hair growth and slows hair loss by stimulating the hair follicles and increasing circulation to the scalp. It's terrific for treating thinning hair and alopecia areata, an autoimmune-related type of hair loss.

Caution: Do not use cedarwood essential oil if you are or might be pregnant.

Rosemary Mint Anti-Frizz Serum

Need to get your mane under control? Try this recipe for an all-natural formula that tames frizzy locks and flyaways without gross chemicals.

Best for:

♥ All hair types, especially ▲ Dry

★ **Superstar ingredient:** Rosemary essential oil is extracted from the leaves of the rosemary bush, which is a member of the mint family, like lavender and sage. It stimulates hair roots, improves circulation and boosts hair growth.

• *Small glass bottle with eyedropper top*

6 tbsp	jojoba oil (see info, page 65)	90 mL
10	drops rosemary essential oil (see Caution, page 91)	10
10	drops peppermint essential oil (see Top tips, page 174)	10

1. Pour jojoba oil, rosemary essential oil and peppermint essential oil into bottle. Shake vigorously until well combined.

2. Shake bottle to recombine before each use. Using eyedropper, place 3 to 5 drops of serum in palm and smooth over damp hair after shampooing and conditioning. Using fingers or a comb, work through to ends. Dry and style hair as usual.

3. Store at room temperature out of direct sunlight for up to 6 months.

DID YOU KNOW? The Ancient Romans often used rosemary (Rosmarinus officinalis) in cooking just like we do, and as a medicinal herb, too, while Ancient Egyptians used it as an incense.

Lavender Luster Serum

The rock-star ingredients in this deep conditioning serum infuse moisture into each and every dry, brittle, damaged strand. The addition of lovely lavender essential oil not only makes this serum smell amazing, but also helps add shine to your tresses.

Best for:

▲ Dry and ≈ Thinning/brittle hair

★ Superstar ingredient:

Avocado oil is lightweight, so it absorbs easily and moisturizes dry hair without giving you limp locks. The vitamin E in avocado oil makes hair stronger, preventing breakage and split ends. It also offers some natural SPF and essential fatty acids that help condition a dry, itchy scalp.

• *Glass bottle with eyedropper top*

¼ cup	jojoba oil (see info, page 65)	60 mL
1 tbsp	avocado oil	15 mL
10	drops lavender essential oil (see info, page 178)	10

1. Pour jojoba oil, avocado oil and lavender essential oil into bottle. Shake vigorously until well combined.

2. Shake bottle to recombine before each use. Using eyedropper, place 3 to 5 drops of serum in palm and smooth over damp, clean hair. Using comb, work through to ends. Style as usual.

3. Store at room temperature out of direct sunlight for up to 6 months.

Essential Oils May Help Hair Growth

Research from the Aberdeen Royal Infirmary in Scotland, published in the medical journal *Archives of Dermatology*, showed that a mix of essential oils can make hair grow back in people with alopecia areata, an autoimmune condition that causes hair to fall out. The study followed 86 people who had been diagnosed with alopecia areata. The participants massaged the bare areas of their scalps for two minutes each evening with a blend of oils: three drops each of lavender and rosemary essential oils, two drops each of thyme and cedarwood essential oils, 4 tsp (20 mL) of grapeseed oil and ¾ tsp (3 mL) of jojoba oil. After the massage, participants wrapped their heads in warm towels to maximize absorption. The results? After seven months, an impressive 44% of the participants experienced hair regrowth. Natural oils for the win!

Lavender Mint No-Poo

Y'all, you do *not* need to wash your hair every day. It's totally OK to skip a day or two, especially if your hair isn't superfine or excessively oily. This DIY dry shampoo recipe will sop up any excess scalp oil between scrubs. This formula is good for all hair colors, but you can dress it up if you have brown, red or pink hair (like me!).

Best for:

♥ All hair types

TOP TIP: Pure cornstarch is gluten-free, but like lots of other ingredients, it can be cross-contaminated during manufacturing. Make sure yours was made in a gluten-free facility.

★ Superstar ingredient: Kaolin clay is a natural, gentle type of earth commonly used in beauty products. It contains tons of silica, which helps to remove dry, dead skin cells. Other minerals and phytonutrients in this clay wipe away toxins and absorb excess oil.

- *Blender*
- *Small glass jar with shaker top*

5 tsp	arrowroot powder or cornstarch	25 mL
2 tsp	kaolin clay	10 mL
5	drops lavender essential oil (see info, page 178)	5
5	drops peppermint essential oil (see Top tips, page 174)	5

1. In blender, combine arrowroot powder, kaolin clay, lavender essential oil and peppermint essential oil. Blend until well combined. Pour into jar.

2. Shake mixture or apply with a clean makeup brush onto roots of dry, unwashed hair. Let stand on hair for a few minutes.

3. Brush hair until all powder is removed.

4. Store at room temperature for up to 6 months.

Variations

Lavender Mint No-Poo for Brunettes
Add unsweetened cocoa powder before blending, using as much or as little as needed to complement your natural hair color.

Lavender Mint No-Poo for Redheads
Add ground cinnamon, rhassoul clay, powdered dried beet root or ground dried hibiscus flowers, using as much or as little as needed to complement your natural hair color.

DID YOU KNOW?
Kaolin clay, also known as white or china clay, is usually found in hot, moist climates. Think tropical rainforests.

Flaxseed Hair-Styling Goop

I always keep a stash of flax seeds in my kitchen. They're nutrient-dense, so I like to add them to smoothies, baked goodies and pretty much everything else. Flax seeds are even packed with good stuff that benefits hair. When boiled, they yield a mega-hold hair jelly that dries quickly and keeps your coif in check.

Best for:

♥ All hair types

TOP TIPS: If you want an even thicker gel, soak the flax seeds in water overnight. Drain them well before combining them with the distilled water in Step 1. Cook as directed. Watch the consistency carefully as the mixture cooks, because it will thicken more quickly.

Don't waste those used flax seeds. Save them to make a batch of Flaxseed Body Scrub (page 150).

★ **Superstar ingredient:** Flax seeds and flaxseed oil are great for your skin and hair, and they're two of the best foods for good health. They contain heart-protecting omega-3 fatty acids that can lower your risk of cardiovascular disease, stroke and diabetes. Flax seeds are also a rich source of lignans, or antioxidant phytoestrogens, that may help reduce your risk of breast and colon cancers. Flax seeds also contain high levels of soluble and insoluble fiber.

- *Fine-mesh sieve*
- *Large glass jar with lid*

2 cups	distilled water	500 mL
1/2 cup	flax seeds	125 mL
1 tsp	vitamin E oil (see Did you know?, page 214)	5 mL
5	drops lavender essential oil (see info, page 178)	5

1. In a large saucepan, combine water and flax seeds. Cook over high heat, stirring constantly, until mixture is the consistency of raw egg whites.

2. Reduce heat to medium. Cook, stirring, for 5 minutes or until thickened to a gel-like consistency. Remove from heat.

3. Place fine-mesh sieve over a large bowl. Strain gel into bowl, pressing with a rubber spatula to extract all gel. Discard seeds or save for another use. Let cool completely.

4. Stir in vitamin E oil and lavender essential oil until well combined. Spoon into jar.

5. Rub or comb goop through damp, clean hair. Dry and style hair as usual.

6. Store in the refrigerator for up to 2 weeks.

DID YOU KNOW?

The beautiful, small, sky-blue-and-white flax flower blooms for just one day — that's it! But each flax plant produces dozens of flowers for three to four weeks. Once the seedpods are ripe, golden and pea-size, the stems are harvested to make fiber (for linen) and the seeds to make oil. It's easy to grow flax in your garden, too. In early spring, plant the seeds in well-drained soil that gets full sun.

Beach Bunny Sea Salt Spray

There's no denying that spending a day at the beach gives you some über-fab wavy, textured hair. If your hair is begging for a tropical vacay, hook it up with some instant, effortless beach waves with this simple recipe.

Best for:

⬤ Normal hair, 💧 Oily hair and ❋ Dandruff-prone hair

★ **Superstar ingredient:** Sea salt is made by evaporating seawater. It's minimally processed, so it contains a treasure trove of nourishing minerals, including sodium, potassium, calcium, magnesium, iron, copper and zinc.

- *Funnel*
- *Glass spray bottle*

1 cup	distilled water	250 mL
1 tbsp	Dead Sea salt (see Caution, below)	15 mL
1 tbsp	aloe vera gel (see info, page 140)	15 mL
15	drops grapefruit essential oil	15
15	drops orange essential oil (see info, page 130)	15

1. In a small saucepan, combine water and Dead Sea salt. Warm over low heat, stirring, for 5 minutes or until salt is dissolved. Remove from heat. Let cool.

2. Stir in aloe vera gel, grapefruit essential oil and orange essential oil until well combined. Using funnel, pour into bottle. Shake vigorously until well combined.

3. Flip head over and spray mixture onto clean, dry hair, using hands to scrunch hair and form waves. Let dry.

4. Store at room temperature for up to 1 month.

Caution: Sea salt can have a drying effect on your hair if you use this mist regularly. But don't sweat it: my Deep Hydration Avocado Hair Mask (page 186) can fix that in no time flat.

Hair Spray-bilizer

Whether you're planning on rocking mad-luscious curls, Farrah Fawcett feathers, a retro beehive, pin curls or subtle waves, you're gonna need hair spray (and lots of it) to stabilize your mane. Ditch the nasty aerosol kind, and make this recipe at home using only two ingredients. If you like scented products, add your favorite essential oil.

Best for:

♥ All hair types

TOP TIP: Adjust the amount of sugar depending on the level of hold you'd like to achieve. More will give you a stronger set; less will yield a softer one.

- *Funnel*
- *Glass spray bottle*

1 cup	filtered water	250 mL
4 tsp	vegan granulated sugar (see Top tip, page 145)	20 mL
4 to 6	drops essential oil of your choice (optional)	4 to 6

1. In a small saucepan, bring water just to a simmer. Stir in sugar until dissolved. Remove from heat. Let cool completely.

2. Stir in essential oil (if using). Using funnel, pour into bottle.

3. Spray mixture over styled hair to set in place.

4. Store at room temperature for up to 2 weeks.

Chapter 7

Makeup and Cosmetics

Makeup Brush Cleaner 200

Luminous Liquid Foundation 201

Flawless Powder Foundation 202

Beauty Balm Cream with SPF 20 204

Fab Finishing Powder 206

Sun-Kissed Bronzer 207

Shimmer Blush 208

Sparkly Illuminating Cream 210

Queen of Egypt Eyeliner 211

Almond Oil Lash-Growth Serum 213

All-Natural Vegan Mascara 214

Spice Girl Shadows 217

Lock-It-In Makeup Setting Spray 218

Luscious Lip Balm 219

Shea Butter Lipstick 220

Tinted Lip Balm 222

Bee-Sting Lip Plumper 223

Lip and Cheek Stain 224

Makeup Brush Cleaner

Before we start, how many of y'all wash your makeup brushes at least a couple times a month? (Crickets chirping.) That's what I thought. With this recipe, you don't need to pay mad stacks for some fancy, packaged brush cleaner. Spotless brushes aren't hospitable to icky bacteria, and they feel nice and fluffy on your face.

Best for:

Grubby makeup brushes

TOP TIP: I'm giving you the ratio of soap to oil here so you can make as big or as little a batch as you like, depending on how many brushes you need to scrub. It's such a simple recipe that you can stir up a fresh batch in seconds.

2	parts unscented liquid castile soap (see Superstar ingredient, page 122)	2
1	part jojoba or olive oil	1

1. In a small bowl, stir castile soap with jojoba oil until well combined.

2. Immerse brush bristles in soap mixture and rub with your fingers until all the gunky buildup comes off.

3. Rinse brush under warm running water, moving the bristles around until the water is no longer sudsy.

4. Gently squeeze out excess water or blot brushes on a clean towel. Let brushes air-dry, preferably hanging them upside down or at an angle so the water doesn't pool and loosen the glue at the base of the bristles.

DID YOU KNOW? Makeup brushes should be cleaned often because they're full of nasty zit-causing grime, such as caked-on makeup, dirt, dead skin cells, bacteria and pore-clogging oils.

DIY Makeup: Gorgeous and Natural

Makeup — aka war paint, spackle (LOL) or whatever you want to call it — is an integral part of my beauty routine. I personally worship makeup because it's fun, it enhances beauty and it makes you feel glam. Most importantly, it empowers people and encourages free expression.

Speaking of empowerment, making your very own custom makeup gives you ultimate control. You can choose every single ingredient that goes on your pretty mug. Your homemade products will contain zero ick-nasties, like toxins, preservatives or artificial this or that. Plus, you can rest assured that no bunnies were harmed in the making of your creative, all-natural cosmetics.

Bonus: every application will cost just pennies, which leaves more funds for your vegan cupcake obsession. (Wait, is that just me?) It's time, compassionate beauty babes, to grab some makeup tools and march over to your kitchen. We're going to get even more gorgeous than we already are!

Luminous Liquid Foundation

Not everyone is a powder foundation junkie like this homegirl (and that's just fine). If you prefer your foundation in liquid form, you can whip up a batch of this dreamy foundation in just a few minutes.

Best for:

● Normal, ▲ Dry,
◆ Sensitive and
■ Mature skin

TOP TIPS: You can also melt the coconut oil in the microwave on High. Do it in 10-second intervals, stirring the oil each time, until it's melted and smooth.

Coconut oil isn't recommended for oily or acne-prone skin. If you make this foundation with jojoba oil, it's suitable for all skin types, including oily.

★ **Superstar ingredient:** Vitamin E is a natural preservative that extends the shelf life of this foundation. It prevents light and air from degrading the active ingredients.

• Small glass jar with lid

2 tbsp	coconut or jojoba oil	30 mL
1 tsp	vitamin E oil	5 mL
1	batch Flawless Powder Foundation (page 202)	1

1. In a small saucepan over low heat, melt coconut oil. Remove from heat. Stir in vitamin E oil until well combined. Let cool.

2. Pour Flawless Powder Foundation into a small bowl. Slowly pour in oil mixture, stirring constantly, until desired consistency is achieved (a thicker consistency makes a terrific concealer). Discard any remaining oil mixture. Spoon foundation into jar.

3. Using finger, makeup sponge or foundation/concealer brush, dot a small amount of foundation on facial skin and blend in.

4. Store at room temperature for up to 6 months.

DID YOU KNOW?

You can highlight your cheekbones and give your face a natural glow (and a model-like look) by smoothing a few dots of coconut oil over top of your makeup.

Flawless Powder Foundation

I lurve natural powder foundation! I've been using it religiously since the early 2000s. Too bad I dropped beaucoup dollarinos on swanky beauty brands for years when I could have been making my own. This is the cheapest and most natural powder you can put on your face: simply arrowroot powder and natural colorants, like the cocoa powder, cinnamon and nutmeg that are waiting in your spice rack.

Best for:

♥ All skin types

TOP TIPS: Lots of beauty-supply stores sell excellent jars designed for storing homemade makeup. For this powder, look for a jar with a built-in sifter top. It will keep any lumps at bay and sprinkle just the right amount of powder on your brush.

You can use a little more or less cocoa, cinnamon or nutmeg to match your skin tone. Play with the amount to find the shade that looks prettiest on you.

★ Superstar ingredient:

Arrowroot powder is a natural starch made from the roots of the tropical South American plant *Maranta arundinacea*. It's white and lightweight, so it's a versatile base for powders and other DIY vegan beauty products.

- *Blender (optional)*
- *Makeup sifter jar*

2 tbsp	arrowroot powder	30 mL
	Powdered natural colorant, such as unsweetened cocoa powder, ground cinnamon or ground nutmeg (see Caution, page 206)	
5	drops lavender essential oil (see Did you know?, page 249)	5

1. In a small bowl, combine arrowroot powder and enough of the colorant to achieve a perfect color match with your skin. Add lavender essential oil. Whisk until well combined. (Alternatively, in blender, combine arrowroot powder, colorant and lavender essential oil. Blend until well combined.)

2. Pour into jar.

3. Sprinkle powder onto a large fluffy makeup brush and apply to facial skin.

4. Store at room temperature for up to 6 months.

DID YOU KNOW?
Arrowroot is aptly named: centuries ago, it was used to treat wounds caused by poisoned arrows.

Beauty Balm Cream with SPF 20

Beauty balms (better known as BB creams) are all the rage these days, and I use them religiously. BB creams are multifunctional: they're an all-in-one solution that plays the roles of a moisturizer, an antiaging serum, a primer, a foundation *and* a sun block. Peeps who can't stand wearing heavy foundation, rejoice!

Best for:

♥ All skin types

TOP TIPS: This beautiful cream is über-versatile. Wear it alone as a tinted moisturizer or a mega-light foundation, or under finishing powder.

If you're antsy and want to cool down your finished cream more quickly, pop it in the fridge for about 30 minutes.

★ **Superstar ingredient:** Mango butter is cold-pressed from the pits inside this tasty fruit. The butter has skin-softening, moisturizing powers, and contains lots of stearic acid, like cocoa butter. It also contains antiaging, wrinkle-fighting, free radical–destroying, antioxidant vitamins A, C and E, plus a healthy dose of nourishing B vitamins and essential minerals. Mango butter is fab at soothing sunburns and easing the uncomfortable symptoms of eczema and psoriasis.

- Tin or glass jar with lid

1½ tbsp	jojoba oil (see info, page 65)	22 mL
1 tbsp	shea butter (see Caution, page 220)	15 mL
1½ tsp	mango butter	7 mL
1½ tsp	candelilla wax (see Did you know?, page 219)	7 mL
1½ tsp	non-nano zinc oxide (see Top tips, page 118)	7 mL
1	drop vitamin E oil	1
	Powdered natural colorant, such as unsweetened cocoa powder, ground cinnamon or ground nutmeg (see Caution, page 206)	

1. Place jojoba oil, shea butter, mango butter and candelilla wax in a small metal or heatproof glass bowl (see Top tips, page 84). Pour enough water into a small saucepan to come about 1½ inches (4 cm) up the side; bring to a simmer. Place bowl on saucepan, making sure the bottom doesn't touch the water. Heat, stirring, for 5 minutes or until jojoba mixture is melted and smooth.

2. Remove bowl from heat. Stir in zinc oxide, vitamin E oil and enough colorant to achieve a perfect color match with your skin. Pour into tin. Let cool completely.

3. Using a makeup sponge or fingers, apply a small amount of cream to facial skin and blend in. Set with your favorite finishing powder.

4. Store at room temperature for up to 2 months.

DID YOU KNOW? Mango trees love hot, wet weather. They grow abundantly in tropical rainforests.

Fab Finishing Powder

My fave makeup product *ever* is finishing powder. It sets my makeup and makes me look like my skin has been Photoshopped (think soft-focus lens or one of those flattering Instagram filters). Makeup companies charge big bucks for this simple beauty product, but you can totally make an awesome vegan version at home, then buy some vegan heels with the dough you saved.

Best for:

♥ All skin types

TOP TIP: Ground cinnamon and cinnamon essential oil bring blood and nutrients to the skin surface, which helps naturally plump the skin and hide fine lines.

- *Blender (optional)*
- *Makeup sifter jar (see Top tips, page 202)*

1 tbsp	arrowroot powder (see info, page 202)	15 mL
	Powdered natural colorant, such as unsweetened cocoa powder or ground cinnamon (see Caution, below)	
3 to 5	drops lavender essential oil (see Did you know?, page 249)	3 to 5

1. In blender, combine arrowroot powder and enough of the colorant to achieve a perfect color match with your skin. Blend until well combined. (Alternatively, in a small bowl, whisk arrowroot powder with colorant until well combined.)

2. Transfer arrowroot mixture to a small bowl. Whisk in lavender essential oil until well combined. Pour into jar.

3. Sprinkle a small amount of powder into jar lid. Press a large fluffy makeup brush into powder and swirl to pick up. Tap brush to remove excess powder. Apply to facial skin.

4. Store at room temperature for up to 6 months.

Caution: Cinnamon can cause burning when applied to the skin, so make sure to avoid the delicate area around your eyes.

Sun-Kissed Bronzer

Want that bronze-goddess glow without the dangers of using tanning salons or roasting in the blazing sun? Me, too! Here's a recipe for DIY bronzer that's cheap, chemical-free, cruelty-free, vegan and easy to make.

Best for:

♥ All skin types

★ Superstar ingredient: Rosemary

is a combo of the Latin words *ros* ("dew") and *marinus* ("seas"), so it means "dew of the seas." This herb is part of the mint family and looks a lot like lavender, with flat, pine-like needles. Both rosemary and lavender essential oils are antibacterial, which means they offer big benefits to acne-prone skin.

- Makeup sifter jar (see Top tips, page 202)

1½ tbsp	unsweetened cocoa powder, divided (see Superstar ingredient, page 104)	22 mL
1 tsp	arrowroot powder, divided (see info, page 202)	5 mL
10 to 15	drops lavender or rosemary essential oil (see Caution, page 91)	10 to 15

1. Pour 1 tbsp (15 mL) of the cocoa powder into a small bowl. Whisk in ½ tsp (2 mL) of the arrowroot powder until well combined.

2. Continue adding remaining cocoa powder and arrowroot powder, a little at a time, until desired shade is achieved (add more cocoa powder to darken, or more arrowroot powder to lighten). Discard any remaining arrowroot powder and cocoa powder. Whisk in lavender essential oil. Pour into jar.

3. Sprinkle bronzer onto a fluffy blush brush and apply to facial skin.

4. Store at room temperature for up to 6 months.

DID YOU KNOW?

Ancient Egyptians, Hebrews, Greeks and Romans considered rosemary a sacred plant. In the Middle Ages, the herb was often used to protect against evil spirits and the plague.

Rosemary and Lavender Beat Stress

Rosemary essential oil is a go-to natural cure for stress. A small study published in the journal *Psychiatry Research* in 2007 showed that subjects who inhaled the aromas of rosemary and lavender essential oils for five minutes had decreased levels of cortisol, a fight-or-flight hormone that's released when we feel stress. Lower cortisol levels are tied to improved immunity.

Shimmer Blush

It's time to talk about your sweet cheeks (the ones upstairs, not your hindquarters). Using blush is a fabulous way to appear youthful and healthy, and this natural option rocks at rosying up your complexion.

Best for:

♥ All skin types

TOP TIP: Make sure your beet root powder is super-duper finely ground, and then grind it some more in a blender. The finer it is, the better it'll adhere to your skin.

★ Superstar ingredient:

Beets contain high levels of antioxidants, vitamins, minerals and micronutrients. Red beets also contain a pigment called betanin, which gives them their bright magenta coloring. In addition to using beet root powder to make blush, you can also use it as natural food coloring.

• *Makeup sifter jar (see Top tips, page 202)*

1 tsp	finely ground beet root powder, alkanet root powder or hibiscus flower powder	5 mL
½ tsp	arrowroot powder (see info, page 202)	2 mL
¼ tsp	unsweetened cocoa powder (see Superstar ingredient, page 104)	1 mL
Pinch	gold mica powder (see Did you know?, page 210)	Pinch
3 to 5	drops lavender essential oil (see Did you know?, page 249)	3 to 5

1. Pour beet root powder into a small bowl. Whisk in arrowroot powder and cocoa powder, a little at a time, until desired shade is achieved. Discard any remaining arrowroot powder and cocoa powder.

2. Whisk in mica powder and lavender essential oil until well combined. Pour into jar.

3. Sprinkle blush onto a fluffy blush brush and apply to cheeks.

4. Store at room temperature for up to 6 months.

Variation
Matte Blush
Omit gold mica for a matte finish.

DID YOU KNOW?
Before dusting blush on your gorgeous mug, apply a bit of the lotion or beauty oil that you normally use — the rosy glow will last longer.

Sparkly Illuminating Cream

It's time to get your sparkle on! Highlighter is one of our secret weapons, ladies. Its light-reflecting, shimmery magic is like nothing short of being kissed by a unicorn.

Best for:

♥ All skin types

TOP TiP: Want a different kind of girlie glow? Swap gold, bronze or copper mica powder for the silver.

• *Small glass jar with lid*

1½ tbsp	Luminous Liquid Foundation (page 201)	22 mL
1 tsp	silver mica powder	5 mL
	Essential oil(s) of your choice (see box, below)	

1. In a small bowl, stir together Luminous Liquid Foundation, mica powder and a few drops of essential oil until well combined. Spoon into jar.

2. Using fingers or a makeup sponge, dab cream down bridge of nose, onto cheekbones, over inner corners of eyes, onto brow bone, in indent above top lip and in middle of forehead. Gently blend in.

3. Store at room temperature for up to 6 months.

DID YOU KNOW? Mica is the name used to refer to minerals that grow in layers. They're crushed into a fine, translucent, shimmery powder that reflects the light — perfect for makeup.

Skin-Loving Essential Oils

Essential oils have a myriad of benefits for the skin. Take a look at what some of my superstar favorites do. If you are or might be pregnant, check the chart on page 54 to see which ones are safe for your use:

- **Basil:** pampers sensitive skin
- **Clary sage:** reduces puffiness
- **Frankincense:** tones and tightens
- **Geranium:** conditions the skin
- **Lavender:** heals skin irritations
- **Lemongrass:** makes skin glow
- **Neroli:** revitalizes mature, aging and sensitive skin
- **Ylang-ylang:** stimulates cell growth

Queen of Egypt Eyeliner

Beauty products used in close proximity to the ol' eyeballs — especially on your waterline — ought to be as natural as possible. You don't want the toxins, preservatives and so on found in mainstream beauty lines sneaking into your system. Your pretty eyes will thank you for using this all-natural, black-as-night eyeliner.

Best for:

♥ All skin types, especially ◆ Sensitive

TOP TIP: You can substitute aloe vera gel, water or melted shea butter for the coconut oil if you want to switch up the consistency of this eyeliner. It's fun to play around and make recipes that specifically cater to your beauty needs, am I right?

• *Small tin or glass jar with lid*

½ tsp	coconut oil	2 mL
3	capsules activated charcoal (see Top tips, page 214)	3

1. Place coconut oil in a small heatproof glass bowl. Microwave on High, stirring every 5 seconds, until melted and completely smooth. (The total time will depend on the strength of your microwave.)

2. Pinch activated charcoal capsules and cut (or twist and pull) halves apart; sprinkle powder over coconut oil. Stir until well combined. Spoon into tin.

3. Using an angled eyeliner brush, gently and carefully line upper and/or lower lids with eyeliner as desired.

4. Store at room temperature for up to 2 months.

Variations

Brown Queen of Egypt Eyeliner
Substitute unsweetened cocoa powder for the charcoal.

Sparkly Queen of Egypt Eyeliner
Add a pinch of gold, silver, bronze or copper mica powder for a bit of sparkle.

Almond Oil Lash-Growth Serum

I wasn't blessed with naturally lush lashes (sigh), so I have long depended on falsies and thickening mascaras to boost my va-va-voominess. However, since I stirred up this growth serum, my lashes definitely look healthier and stronger. Yours will, too!

Best for:

▲ Dry, brittle or thin lashes

TOP TiP: Almond oil also helps banish dark under-eye circles and puffiness. Gently massage a few drops into the skin around your eyes. Do this twice a day, in the morning and at night, for excellent results.

★ **Superstar ingredient:** Castor oil boosts blood circulation, which encourages faster hair growth. It's also rich in vitamin E and proteins.

• *Small glass bottle with eyedropper top*

1 tbsp	castor oil	15 mL
1 tbsp	sweet almond oil	15 mL
5	drops vitamin E oil (see Did you know?, page 214)	5

1. In a small bowl, stir together castor oil, sweet almond oil and vitamin E oil until well combined. Pour into bottle.

2. Using eyedropper, place 2 or 3 drops of serum on fingertips and massage between fingers. Spread over lashes to coat. (Or drop oil onto a clean mascara wand and apply to lashes.) Repeat daily, preferably just before bed.

3. Store at room temperature for up to 6 months.

All-Natural Vegan Mascara

Most mainstream mascaras contain not-so-sexy, toxic ingredients, such as 2-propanol, butylated hydroxyanisole, butylated hydroxytoluene, propylene glycol, parabens, phthalates and aluminum. Seriously, how is it legal for companies to sell such nasty stuff for your eyes? Skip all those and try this all-natural mascara that actually *works*.

Best for:

♥ All skin types, especially ◆ Sensitive

TOP TiPS: You'll find activated charcoal near all the other supplements at the health food store. When you buy supplement capsules, like the activated charcoal, always make sure they're vegan (no gross gelatin!) and gluten-free. Lots of supplements contain these additives, so it pays to read the label before you buy.

Activated charcoal is messy and may stain fabric. Wear something you don't care about when making this recipe.

To make your lashes even more va-va-voomy: curl them with an eyelash curler, and then apply one or two coats of mascara in an upward motion, going from roots to tips. With a cotton swab, carefully pat your lashes with arrowroot powder or cornstarch to set them. Apply another coat of mascara and you're ready to go.

- *Small oral syringe*
- *Mascara tube*

10	capsules activated charcoal	10
2 tsp	aloe vera gel (see info, page 140)	10 mL
1/8 tsp	vitamin E oil	0.5 mL
Pinch	bentonite clay	Pinch

1. Pinch activated charcoal capsules and cut (or twist and pull) halves apart; sprinkle powder into a small bowl. Discard capsules.

2. Stir in aloe vera gel, vitamin E oil and bentonite clay until completely smooth.

3. Insert tip of oral syringe into charcoal mixture and pull the plunger to suck up the mixture. Insert into mascara tube and press the plunger to fill.

4. Apply mascara to lashes, using several coats if desired and letting dry between coats.

5. Store at room temperature for up to 2 months.

DID YOU KNOW?

Vitamin E oil is a natural preservative. You can buy bottles of it, or just bust open a capsule (again, veggie, not gelatin!) and squeeze out the oil.

Spice Girl Shadows

Powdered algae, charcoal and spices — do those sound like ingredients for beauteous eyes? They should! These all-natural, vegan colorants are just the thing to enhance your peepers. March your cutie patootie to the kitchen right now and grab some eyeshadow brushes on the way.

Best for:

♥ All skin types

TOP TiPS: Arrowroot and cornstarch function in similar ways, but cornstarch is highly processed and often made from genetically modified corn. Arrowroot is a more-natural, less-processed alternative that works well in many recipes.

The shea butter adds a bit of moisture to this shadow and helps it stay put on your lids.

★ **Superstar ingredient:** Spirulina is a natural algae powder that will give your shadow a green hue. It's about 60% protein, and rich in antioxidants, vitamins and minerals; it is often consumed by vegetarians and vegans because it is high in bioavailable iron. Look for spirulina in the vitamin section of health food stores, and be sure to buy an organic brand. Conventionally harvested spirulina may be contaminated with toxins or contain chemical additives.

• *Small tin or glass jar with lid*

½ tsp	arrowroot powder	2 mL
½ tsp	powdered natural colorant(s), see box, below	2 mL
½ tsp	shea butter (see Caution, page 220)	2 mL

1. In a small bowl, whisk arrowroot powder with natural colorant(s), adding a little of each at a time, until desired shade is achieved. Discard any remaining arrowroot powder and natural colorants.

2. Using a fork, mash in shea butter until well combined and as smooth as possible. Spoon into tin.

3. Using an eyeshadow brush, apply shadow on eyelids.

4. Store at room temperature for up to 6 months.

Natural Eyeshadow Colorant Options

The only limitation on this recipe is your imagination. You can stir up DIY eyeshadows in a million hues with these all-natural options:

• **Black:** activated charcoal powder (see Top tips, page 214)

• **Brown:** unsweetened cocoa powder, ground cinnamon and ground nutmeg (see Caution, page 206)

• **Green:** spirulina powder

• **Pink or red:** beet root powder, hibiscus flower powder or sweet paprika

• **Yellow:** turmeric (see Superstar ingredient, page 108)

DID YOU KNOW? Spirulina is chock-full of chlorophyll, which helps remove toxins from the body.

Lock-It-In Makeup Setting Spray

If you want your makeup to last for hours — and are looking to lock in some extra moisture, too — there's nothing like an all-natural setting spray to get the job done. You can also use this spray to freshen up your makeup throughout the day.

Best for:

♥ All skin types, especially ▲ Dry and ◆ Sensitive

★ **Superstar ingredient:** Vegetable glycerin is extracted from seed oils: palm kernels, soybeans and coconuts. It's a mega-common ingredient in DIY vegan beauty recipes because it's moisturizing and easily absorbed by the skin, and contains no icky animal products. Look for pharmaceutical-quality brands made from non-GMO ingredients that carry the logo of the U.S. Pharmacopeial Convention (USP), a nonprofit organization that measures ingredient purity.

• *Small glass spray bottle*

3 tbsp	Rose Water Toner for Dry or Sensitive Skin (page 80)	45 mL
1 tbsp	liquid vegetable glycerin	15 mL
5	drops lavender essential oil (see Did you know?, page 249)	5

1. Pour Rose Water Toner, vegetable glycerin and lavender essential oil into bottle. Shake vigorously until well combined.

2. Shake bottle to recombine before each use. Spray mixture all over facial skin after applying makeup. Let dry.

3. Store in the refrigerator for up to 2 weeks.

Luscious Lip Balm

I'm a lip balm addict. I can't go a single minute without having my smackers balmed-up, even while I'm snoozing. And I lurve making my own. Not only am I in control of the ingredients (no beeswax, aka definitely-not-vegan bee secretions), but also, I can make a batch of three balms at one time.

Best for:

♥ All skin types, especially ▲ Dry

★ Superstar ingredient:

Coconut oil is beneficial for skin and hair, and it's a superfood. It's high in antioxidants and fatty acids that give it powerful medicinal properties. Consuming it is good for your heart, digestion and immunity. It's also one of nature's best moisturizers, so it's the bomb for healing chapped lips caused by cold, dry weather.

• *3 lip balm tubes or tins*

1 tbsp	candelilla wax	15 mL
1 tbsp	coconut oil	15 mL
¼ tsp	shea butter (see Caution, page 220)	1 mL
5 to 10	drops peppermint or sweet orange essential oil	5 to 10

1. In a small heatproof glass measuring cup, combine candelilla wax, coconut oil and shea butter. Microwave on High, stirring every 10 seconds, until melted and completely smooth. (The total time will depend on the strength of your microwave.)

2. Stir in peppermint essential oil. Immediately pour into lip balm tubes. Refrigerate for 30 minutes or until completely cooled and firm.

3. Apply balm to lips as often as you like.

4. Store at room temperature for up to 6 months.

DID YOU KNOW?
Candelilla wax is a vegan beauty hero because it's an effective plant-based alternative to beeswax. It actually makes lip balms smoother and creamier than beeswax does.

Shea Butter Lipstick

Tons of conventional lipsticks contain toxic heavy metals, including lead. Lead! And if that weren't shocking enough, many are dyed with cochineal, or crushed beetles! Eeeeeeeew. Since we all unintentionally eat lipstick throughout the day or during the course of a meal, let's consume only the pure, natural, bug-free stuff from now on, OK?

Best for:

♥ All skin types, especially ▲ Dry

TOP TIP: You can bump up the amount of pink or red mica to a max of 1 tbsp (15 mL) if you want a more intense shade.

★ Superstar ingredient: Shea butter is rich in essential fatty acids, phytosterols (phyto = plant), vitamins D and E, provitamin A and allantoin, which protects your skin from the sun's UV rays, pollution, harsh weather and dehydration. Shea butter also heals minor skin problems, including cuts and burns.

• *2 lip balm tubes or tins*

1 tsp	shea butter (see Caution, below) or cocoa butter, grated (see Top tips, page 84)	5 mL
1 tsp	jojoba, sweet almond, coconut or olive oil	5 mL
¾ tsp	candelilla wax (see Did you know?, page 219)	3 mL
1 tsp	pink or red mica	5 mL
3 to 5	drops peppermint essential oil (see Did you know?, page 123)	3 to 5

1. In a small heatproof glass measuring cup or bowl, combine shea butter, jojoba oil and candelilla wax. Microwave on High, stirring every 10 seconds, until melted and completely smooth. (The total time will depend on the strength of your microwave.)

2. Stir in mica and peppermint essential oil until well combined. Immediately pour into lip balm tubes. Refrigerate for 30 minutes or until completely cooled and firm.

3. Apply balm to lips as often as you like.

4. Store at room temperature for up to 6 months.

Caution: Nut allergies? Check with your physician before applying shea butter.

DID YOU KNOW?

Shea butter comes from the nuts (actually the seeds) of the shea tree, which grows on the savannas in Western Africa. The shea tree is considered sacred and flowers only once it's about 20 years old. Some trees live for up to 200 years!

Tinted Lip Balm

If you're like me and you're constantly looking for makeup shortcuts, you'll love this tinted lip balm. It delivers a subtle hint of color with mega-moisture, perfect for days you might be a little too lazy to apply full-on lipstick.

Best for:

♥ All skin types, especially ▲ Dry

★ **Superstar ingredient:** Alkanet root powder is made from the red roots of the *Alkanna tinctoria* plant, which has pretty violet flowers. Alkanet root is often used to color soaps and as a natural dye for clothing; it can produce a range of colors, from purple to blue to pinky-red, depending on the pH it's exposed to. It's also commonly added to lipsticks to give them a reddish color.

• *2 lip balm tubes or tins*

1 tbsp	coconut oil (see Superstar ingredient, page 219)	15 mL
1 tsp	candelilla wax (see Did you know?, page 219)	5 mL
¼ tsp	alkanet root powder or beet root powder	1 mL
1	drop vitamin E oil	1

1. In a small heatproof glass measuring cup, combine coconut oil and candelilla wax. Microwave on High, stirring every 10 seconds, until melted and completely smooth. (The total time will depend on the strength of your microwave.)

2. Stir in alkanet root powder and vitamin E oil until well combined. Immediately pour into lip balm tubes. Refrigerate for 30 minutes or until completely cooled and firm.

3. Apply balm to lips as often as you like.

4. Store at room temperature for up to 6 months.

DID YOU KNOW?
Oil infused with alkanet root is a soothing emollient for itchy, inflamed or irritated skin. It's terrific for checking the symptoms of eczema and acne. Alkanet ointments are astringent and antimicrobial, so they can help treat minor wounds.

Bee-Sting Lip Plumper

All right, who's ready for a mega-plump, bee-stung, Angelina Jolie–style pout? I'm guessing you (and me!). It's crazy-simple to make this plumper, and you're not going to spend mad stacks on fancy-pants brands. Cinnamon essential oil helps this lippie give you a sexy smoocher.

Best for:

♥ All skin types

TOP TIPS: True cinnamon bark essential oil is made from the inner bark of the Ceylon cinnamon plant, *Cinnamomum zeylanicum*; cinnamon leaf essential oil is made from the leaves. Another option is the essential oil made from the similar *Cinnamomum cassia*, or Chinese cinnamon, plant. These oils plump up lips by gently irritating the mucous membranes and increasing blood flow. They also give your lips a sweet, kissable scent.

This lip balm is OK for all skin types, but if you have sensitive skin, you may want to avoid using it too often. Skip it if your skin is irritated.

• *Small glass bottle with roll-on top*

2 tbsp	sweet almond or jojoba oil	30 mL
10	drops cinnamon essential oil (see Caution, below)	10
2	drops vitamin E oil	2

1. Pour sweet almond oil, cinnamon essential oil and vitamin E oil into bottle. Shake vigorously until well combined.

2. Shake bottle to recombine before each use. Roll plumper onto lips as often as you like.

3. Store at room temperature for up to 6 months.

DID YOU KNOW? Inhaling the aroma of cinnamon essential oil can relieve the nausea that accompanies motion sickness.

Caution: Do not use cinnamon essential oil if you are or might be pregnant.

Lip and Cheek Stain

This dainty, sheer stain is super-easy to make and gives you the sweetest hint of a flush. Use it and you'll look like a cutie just told you how *fine* you are! Before you start, grab some disposable gloves, because the main ingredient can get a little messy.

Best for:

● Normal, ▲ Dry,
◐ Combination and
■ Mature skin

TOP TiP: Cooking the beet before puréeing it helps maximize the color payout.

★ Superstar ingredient:
Beets give cosmetics a natural pink hue, and they're so good for you. Drinking beet juice can protect your liver, and boost your energy and stamina. It's full of naturally occurring nitrate, which increases the body's supply of nitric oxide, a molecule in blood vessels that improves circulation to the brain, heart and muscles. Working with other phytonutrients, beet juice can help lower blood pressure.

- *Blender or food processor*
- *Fine-mesh sieve (optional)*
- *Small tin or glass jar with lid*

1	small beet, scrubbed (see Caution, below)	1
2 tbsp	coconut oil (see Superstar ingredient, page 219)	30 mL
1 tsp	freshly squeezed lemon juice	5 mL
2	drops vitamin E oil	2

1. In a small saucepan of boiling water, cook beet for 20 to 30 minutes or until fork-tender. Drain, peel and cut beet into small chunks.

2. In blender, combine beet, coconut oil, lemon juice and vitamin E oil. Blend until smooth.

3. Place fine-mesh sieve (if using) over a small bowl and strain beet mixture into bowl, pressing with a rubber spatula. (You can skip this step if you don't mind the stain a little gritty.) Pour into tin. Let cool completely.

4. Using a lip brush, apply stain all over lips (or using finger, rub onto cheeks).

5. Store in the refrigerator for up to 1 month.

Caution: If you want to try beet juice to treat high blood pressure, do it with your doctor's guidance. And never adjust your medications without seeking medical advice.

DID YOU KNOW?
Beet juice is a powerful detoxifier, so add it to your diet gradually. Start with ¼ cup (60 mL) per day and slowly work up to 1 to 2 cups (250 to 500 mL) daily.

Chapter 8

Unisex Beauty Essentials

Baking Soda–Free Spray Deodorant 229

Vanilla Dusting Powder. 231

Keep-It-Dry Deodorant Paste 232

Refresh-Your-Breath Minty Mouthwash 234

Charcoal Natural Tooth Whitener 235

Peppermint Toothpaste 236

Strawberry Natural Tooth Whitener 239

Coconut-Shea Smooth-Shave Cream 240

Witch Hazel Aftershave 242

Lemon Eucalyptus and Citronella Bug Repellent 245

Sweet Almond Hand Cream 246

TLC Cuticle Oil 248

Lavender Hand Sanitizer 249

DETOX YOUR PITS

Congrats! You've chucked your antiperspirant in the trash and decided to switch to natural deodorant. Now what?

First, you'll need to detox your pits. Why? Because natural deodorants will work more effectively if you start with a clean slate. Most store-bought antiperspirants use aluminum-based compounds to plug up sweat glands, so your body will have to get rid of this buildup. These chemicals have been linked to lots of different health concerns, including Alzheimer's disease, so it's wise in the long run to reduce your exposure to them. Plus, the human body is meant to sweat. It's a natural function, and an essential way for the body to release waste materials and toxins from the skin.

When you switch from antiperspirant to natural deodorant, your glands and pores will start to unclog and work properly again. As your body starts to adjust to the new regimen, it will purge toxins and other accumulated gunk (dead skin cells, chemical residues and so on). This may temporarily cause you to be … well … more aromatic than usual. But don't give up and switch back to antiperspirant, no matter how tempting it is. This change just means that you're detoxing; your ramped-up fragrance will last only about a week, and it's well worth getting through. Hint: staying hydrated and exercising can help speed up this transition time.

Once you've made it through the transition and cleaned the slate, the best way to keep underarm odor in check is to kill the bacteria that breed there. And in this chapter, you've got the tools to make that happen: all-natural, vegan, cruelty-free deodorants, made at home with love.

Not So Natural After All

Even some "natural" deodorants you'll find at the health food store contain questionable chemical ingredients (see pages 28 to 31 for more on some of the worst offenders). Make sure you read ingredient lists and skip any product that contains potentially harmful ingredients, such as the following:

- Fragrance
- Imidazolidinyl urea
- Octoxynol and nonoxynol
- Parabens

- Propylene glycol
- Synthetic colors
- Triclosan
- Triethanolamine (TEA)

Baking Soda–Free Spray Deodorant

There's no need to spend your precious, hard-earned cheddar on deodorants now that you can make simple ones like this from scratch. This spray-on formula is baking soda–free, so it's especially great for people with sensitive skin. Spritz it on and go enjoy a beautiful, non-stanky day.

Best for:

♥ All skin types, especially ◆ Sensitive

TOP TiP: When you're choosing essential oil(s) for this recipe, try the odor-fighting options I've mentioned in the Top tip on page 232. One of my favorites to add to this spray deodorant is sweet orange essential oil, because it's antibacterial, antifungal, anti-inflammatory and antiseptic. It'll also help your skin detox itself naturally.

- *Glass spray bottle*

2 oz	witch hazel (see Superstar ingredient, page 242)	60 g
12	drops essential oil(s) of your choice	12

1. Pour witch hazel and essential oil(s) into bottle. Shake vigorously until well combined.

2. Shake bottle to recombine before each use. Spray over underarms. Let dry.

3. Store at room temperature for up to 3 months.

Put the Personal in Personal Care

The last thing you want is for toxic chemicals to creep into the products you use the most, such as toothpaste and deodorant. You use them every day (multiple times a day in some cases), so it's high time you detox your beauty routine. By ditching cheap, store-bought, chemical-laden junk, you'll lower your exposure to all that nasty stuff and open the door to healthy ingredients. When you churn out batches of wholesome, awesome, truly good-for-you personal-care products, you're loving your body and the Earth. You control what goes into each formula, and your teeth, pits and other lovable bits will thank you kindly.

DID YOU KNOW?
If you feel anxious or have mild depression, try taking 8 to 10 deep inhalations over a bottle of sweet orange essential oil (or put it in a room diffuser). The aroma can help make you feel happier and more optimistic.

Vanilla Dusting Powder

We all get a little schvitzy sometimes. There's no such thing as a body deodorant per se, so I'm all about dusting powders, especially the vanilla variety. I adore vanilla more than anyone you'll ever meet, guaranteed. One of my life goals is to always smell like a vanilla sugar cookie, and this recipe sets me up for success! Want a more neutral or more masculine scent? Omit the vanilla and dress up the powder with your favorite essential oils.

Best for:

♥ All skin types

TOP TiPS: Add a little bit of gold, silver, bronze or copper mica if you want to give your powder a subtle sparkling effect.

You can add a little more or a little less vanilla powder, depending on your love for its fragrance.

★ **Superstar ingredient:** Baking soda is antifungal and antiseptic, so it's a natural deodorizer. It also absorbs moisture from the skin and keeps it dry.

Caution: Baking soda is a super-safe ingredient to use. Unfortunately, though, some people have sensitive skin that reacts to it. The good news: just leave it out of this recipe if it doesn't work for you.

• Makeup sifter jar (see Top tips, page 202)

1 cup	arrowroot powder or white rice flour	250 mL
2 tbsp	baking soda (see Caution, below)	30 mL
1 tbsp	vanilla powder (see info, page 151)	15 mL

1. In a small bowl, whisk together arrowroot powder, baking soda and vanilla powder. Pour into jar.

2. Dust into shoes, onto feet or underarms, or over any other high-perspiration areas.

3. Store at room temperature for up to 1 year.

DID YOU KNOW? When it comes to aromatherapy, vanilla is just the ticket for calming; relaxing; lifting your mood; and reducing stress, anger, tension and irritability.

Keep-It-Dry Deodorant Paste

Tired of searching for a pure, chemical-free deodorant that doesn't cost a fortune? Yeah, me, too. Here's a mega-simple DIY deodorant that focuses on safe, effective ingredients. No muss, no fuss, no stink!

Best for:

● Normal,
◑ Combination,
● Oily/acne-prone,
▲ Dry and ■ Mature skin

TOP TIP: Tea tree, lavender and lemongrass essential oils are all powerful odor fighters. Add a few drops and you'll be smelling sweet!

★ Superstar ingredient: Coconut oil is a terrific emollient. It was also popular for cooking in the United States and Canada until the 1970s, when corn and soy oil companies ramped up their propaganda against it. They claimed that its high saturated fat content made it dangerous to consume, but today, we know that coconut oil is more complex than that. The saturated fat in coconut oil consists primarily of medium-chain fatty acids, which aren't as easily stored as fat by the body.

• *Small glass jar with lid*

3 tbsp	arrowroot powder or cornstarch	45 mL
1 tbsp	baking soda (see Caution, page 231) or kaolin clay	15 mL
2 tbsp	coconut oil	30 mL
5	drops essential oil(s) of your choice	5

1. In a small bowl, whisk arrowroot powder with baking soda until well combined. Set aside.

2. Place coconut oil in a small heatproof glass bowl. Microwave on High, stirring every 5 seconds, until melted and completely smooth. (The total time will depend on the strength of your microwave.)

3. Whisk coconut oil into arrowroot mixture along with essential oil(s) until a paste forms. Pour into jar.

4. Using fingers, rub a small amount of paste over underarm skin until absorbed.

5. Store at room temperature for up to 1 year.

DID YOU KNOW? Some studies have shown that including coconut oil in your diet can boost HDL (good cholesterol), improve insulin sensitivity in people with type 2 diabetes and help you lose weight.

Refresh-Your-Breath Minty Mouthwash

Most mainstream mouthwashes contain funky ingredients, such as sodium lauryl sulfate, phthalates, parabens, artificial sweeteners, and synthetic dyes and flavors. Do you really want to get your swish on with all that unnatural stuff? Well, now you don't have to expose yourself to toxins to get minty fresh.

Best for:

Healthy teeth and gums

TOP TIP: You don't have to make your mouthwash sweet, but it can make the experience a little less bracing. Xylitol is a natural sugar alcohol found in fruits; it is processed into a powder that you can add to liquids. If you don't want to use or can't find xylitol powder, you can substitute a pinch of stevia.

• *Glass bottle with lid*

1 cup	filtered water	250 mL
¼ cup	witch hazel (see Superstar ingredient, page 242)	60 mL
1 tbsp	baking soda (see Superstar ingredient, page 236)	15 mL
½ tsp	xylitol powder (optional)	2 mL
12	drops peppermint essential oil (see Did you know?, page 123)	12

1. Pour water, witch hazel, baking soda, xylitol powder (if using) and peppermint essential oil into bottle. Shake vigorously until well combined and dry ingredients are dissolved.

2. Shake bottle to recombine before each use. Swish 1 to 2 tsp (5 to 10 mL) of mouthwash in mouth for about 1 minute after brushing teeth. Spit out and rinse mouth with water.

3. Store in the refrigerator for up to 2 weeks.

DID YOU KNOW?

Stevia is a small green plant that's native to Paraguay. It contains steviol glycosides, natural plant compounds that make it much, much sweeter than sugar. The leaves contain protein, fiber, carbohydrates, vitamins A and C, and minerals such as iron and zinc. You can use stevia as a sugar substitute in tea, coffee and many of your favorite vegan recipes.

Charcoal Natural Tooth Whitener

Sometimes you gotta get dirty before you can get clean. This treatment will make your mouth look crazy-black, but when it's rinsed off, you'll have gleaming teeth that are worth smiling about. Charcoal may stain fabric, so wear an old shirt in case you dribble.

Best for:

Healthy teeth and gums

TOP TIP: When you buy supplement capsules, like the activated charcoal here, always make sure they're vegan (no gross gelatin!) and gluten-free. Lots of supplements contain these additives, so it pays to read the label before you buy.

★ Superstar ingredient: Activated charcoal is porous and has natural adhesive qualities, so it binds to tannins in teeth-staining culprits like coffee, tea, wine and certain foods.

2	capsules activated charcoal (see Caution, below)	2
	Filtered water	

1. Pinch activated charcoal capsules and cut (or twist and pull) halves apart; sprinkle powder into a small bowl.

2. Stir in water, a little bit at a time, until a paste forms.

3. Using finger, gently rub paste all over teeth to coat. Let stand on teeth for 3 to 5 minutes.

4. Rinse mouth with water. Brush teeth with your favorite toothpaste to remove any residue.

Caution: Since this is a treatment you're going to put in your mouth, make sure you buy activated charcoal, which is safe for consumption. You'll find the activated charcoal near all the other supplements at the health food store.

Peppermint Toothpaste

When it comes to products you put in your mouth (and therefore ingest), you definitely want to steer clear of chemicals and unpronounceable ingredients. There is so much of that nasty stuff in conventional toothpastes, so trade them in for this DIY one that gets your whites looking their pearliest without all that extra yuck.

Best for:

Healthy teeth and gums

★ **Superstar ingredient:** Baking soda naturally whitens and brightens your smile. The alkaline properties of baking soda also prevent acid from damaging your tooth enamel.

- Glass jar with lid

⅓ cup	baking soda	75 mL
1 tsp	fine sea salt (see Superstar ingredient, page 196)	5 mL
1	packet stevia (optional), see Did you know?, page 234	1
15	drops peppermint essential oil	15
	Coconut oil (see info, page 232)	

1. In a small bowl, stir together baking soda, sea salt, stevia (if using) and peppermint essential oil until well combined.

2. Mash in coconut oil, a little at a time, until a paste forms and the mixture is the desired consistency. Spoon into jar.

3. Dip a clean toothbrush into toothpaste. Moisten with water and brush teeth. Rinse mouth with water.

4. Store at room temperature for up to 6 months.

DID YOU KNOW?
Peppermint essential oil kicks ass in toothpaste because it's antiseptic and antimicrobial. It cleans up teeth, kills bacteria and gives you fresh-smelling breath.

Strawberry Natural Tooth Whitener

Think whitening your teeth has to involve gross chemical bleaches? Not so! Get ready to swap out your conventional teeth-whitening trays, gels and strips in favor of this all-natural treatment. Make sure you try my other fun, fruity option, too (see box, below).

Best for:

Healthy teeth and gums

★ Superstar ingredient:

Strawberries contain malic acid, which helps remove tooth discolorations caused by everyday eating and drinking.

- Mortar and pestle (optional)

½   small ripe strawberry, hulled and halved   ½

Baking soda (see Caution, below)

1. In mortar with pestle (or on a small plate and using a fork), mash strawberry. Stir in enough baking soda to make a paste.

2. Dip a clean toothbrush into whitener. Brush all over teeth. Let stand on teeth for 3 to 5 minutes.

3. Rinse mouth with water. Brush teeth with your favorite toothpaste to remove any residue.

Banana Peels Whiten Teeth, Too

There's plenty of anecdotal evidence that you can use a banana peel to whiten your teeth. And why not try it? Bananas contain lots of potassium, magnesium and manganese, which are great for your choppers. Grab a fresh, ripe banana and peel it (the fruit is great for you, so dig in!). Now rub the inside of the peel all over your teeth. Let the banana residue work its magic on your teeth for a couple of minutes, then rinse and brush as usual. Try this treatment a couple of times a week for a month or so, and you'll have a brighter smile.

Caution: This treatment can be a bit abrasive, so I recommend you use it once or twice a week at most.

Coconut-Shea Smooth-Shave Cream

Y'all, get ready for the closest shave of your life. With no unnecessary perfumes, chemicals or less-than-healthy ingredients, this DIY shaving cream is super-nourishing and moisturizing. It'll leave you with the silkiest, most kissable skin ever — for just pocket change.

Best for:

● Normal,
◐ Combination,
▲ Dry, ◆ Sensitive
and ■ Mature skin

TOP TIP: Chamomile is antibacterial, antifungal, anti-inflammatory and antiseptic. It's also hypoallergenic, making it gentle for people with sensitive skin.

★ Superstar ingredient: Cold-pressed (raw) organic coconut oil contains tons of vitamins and minerals, and is high in fatty acids, especially lauric and caprylic acid, which are antibacterial. All of these help protect skin cell membranes.

- Hand mixer
- Jar with lid

⅓ cup	coconut oil	75 mL
⅓ cup	shea butter (see Caution, page 220)	75 mL
¼ cup	jojoba oil (see Did you know?, page 248)	60 mL
5	drops lavender essential oil (see Did you know?, page 249)	5
5	drops chamomile essential oil	5

1. Place coconut oil and shea butter in a small metal or heatproof glass bowl (see Top tips, page 84). Pour enough water into a small saucepan to come about 1½ inches (4 cm) up the side; bring to a simmer. Place bowl on saucepan, making sure the bottom doesn't touch the water. Heat, stirring, for 5 to 10 minutes or until coconut oil mixture is melted and smooth.

2. Remove bowl from heat. Stir in jojoba oil, lavender essential oil and chamomile essential oil. Refrigerate for 30 minutes or until thickened.

3. Remove bowl from refrigerator. Using hand mixer, beat for 2 to 3 minutes or until creamy. Spoon into jar.

4. Using fingers or a shaving brush, spread cream over skin and shave. Rinse skin with warm water and pat dry with a towel. Follow with your favorite body moisturizer.

5. Store in the shower for up to 6 months.

DID YOU KNOW?
Coconut oil has a natural SPF of 8 to 10, so it can help protect skin against UV damage.

Witch Hazel Aftershave

Fellas love this potion. Witch hazel tightens and tones pores post-shave, keeping out dirt and excess oil, and preventing irritation. This recipe is also antimicrobial, meaning it kills bacteria so any nicks or cuts won't get infected. Plus, the fresh peppermint scent will give your man a nice wake-up call.

Best for:

⬤ Normal,
◑ Combination and
⬤ Oily/acne-prone skin

★ Superstar ingredient:
Witch hazel is an old-fashioned, natural remedy your granny probably kept in her medicine cupboard. And she was right! You can use it for tons of natural treatments; it's astringent and a gentle antibacterial agent, so it shrinks pores, cleanses skin and fights acne.

- *Small funnel*
- *Glass spray bottle*

⅓ cup	witch hazel	75 mL
2 tbsp	liquid vegetable glycerin (see Superstar ingredient, page 218)	30 mL
15	drops rosemary essential oil (see Caution, page 91)	15
15	drops peppermint essential oil	15

1. Using funnel, pour witch hazel, vegetable glycerin, rosemary essential oil and peppermint essential oil into bottle. Shake vigorously until well combined.

2. Shake bottle to recombine before each use. Spray aftershave directly onto facial skin or spray into palm and pat over facial skin after shaving.

3. Store at room temperature for up to 6 months.

DID YOU KNOW?
Researchers at Wheeling Jesuit University in West Virginia found that when study participants smelled the aromas of peppermint and cinnamon for 30 seconds every 15 minutes during a simulated driving experiment, they were more alert, less anxious and frustrated, and felt less tired.

Lemon Eucalyptus and Citronella Bug Repellent

When I was a wee tot, my mama always told me I had sweet blood because insects liked to bite me… a lot! To this day, I'm a bug magnet. But I've traded store-bought, chemical-laced bug spray for my own easy-peasy nontoxic repellent. Trust me, it works, even on sweet-blooded people like me.

Best for:

♥ All skin types

TOP TiP: The essential oil made from the leaves and twigs of the lemon eucalyptus tree (*Eucalyptus citriodora* or *Corymbia citriodora*) has a fresh lemony-herbal scent, and is often added to natural bug repellents.

★ **Superstar ingredient:** A study conducted at the London School of Hygiene and Tropical Medicine in 2002 showed that bug repellent made with lemon eucalyptus oil (which contains 30% of the active component p-menthane-diol) was 96.89% effective at repelling mosquitos for a four-hour period. It handily beat out the chemical DEET (found in many commercial chemical repellents), which provided only 84.81% protection over the same period.

Caution: Do not use lemon eucalyptus or citronella essential oil if you are or might be pregnant.

- *Glass spray bottle*

2 tbsp	witch hazel (see Superstar ingredient, page 242)	30 mL
2 tbsp	jojoba oil (see Did you know?, page 248)	30 mL
½ tsp	vitamin E oil (see Did you know?, page 214)	2 mL
50	drops lemon eucalyptus essential oil (see Caution, below)	50
15	drops lavender essential oil (see Did you know?, page 249)	15
15	drops citronella essential oil (see Caution, below)	15

1. Pour witch hazel, jojoba oil, vitamin E oil, and lemon eucalyptus, lavender and citronella essential oils into bottle. Shake until well combined.

2. Shake bottle vigorously to recombine before each use. Spray bug repellent directly onto skin or spray into palm and pat over skin, especially in delicate areas, such as around the eyes and mouth.

3. Store at room temperature for up to 6 months.

Sweet Almond Hand Cream

Soothe your dry, chapped paws with this luxe moisturizing cream. It's packed with nourishing all-natural oils that your skin will happily slurp right up.

Best for:

♥ All skin types, especially ▲ Dry

TOP TiP: Coconut oil, when consumed regularly, gives skin an even tone and reduces the size of pores. It also boosts immunity and energy levels. Coconut oil contains important fatty acids (capric, carprylic and lauric acids) that have disinfectant and antimicrobial properties. These protect your skin from infection. Coconut also contains a small amount of antioxidant vitamin E, which helps protect the skin from free radical damage.

★ **Superstar ingredient:** Sweet almond oil has high levels of fatty acids that act as a natural emollient for the skin. It is an excellent addition to hand creams.

• *Glass jar with lid*

3 tbsp	candelilla wax	45 mL
2 tbsp	coconut oil	30 mL
⅓ cup	sweet almond oil	75 mL
2 tbsp	jojoba oil (see Did you know?, page 248)	30 mL
20	drops lavender essential oil (see Did you know?, page 249)	20

1. Place candelilla wax and coconut oil in a small metal or heatproof glass bowl (see Top tips, page 84). Pour enough water into a small saucepan to come about 1½ inches (4 cm) up the side; bring to a simmer. Place bowl on saucepan, making sure the bottom doesn't touch the water. Heat, stirring, for 5 to 10 minutes or until wax mixture is melted and smooth.

2. Remove bowl from heat. Stir in sweet almond oil, jojoba oil and lavender essential oil until creamy. Spoon into jar. Let cool until solidified.

3. Rub a small amount all over hands, focusing on dry spots. Repeat as often as desired.

4. Store at room temperature for up to 6 months.

DID YOU KNOW?

Candelilla wax is made from the natural coating on the stems of the shrub *Euphorbia cerifera*, which is native to Mexico and the southwestern United States. The wax coating on the stems keeps the plant hydrated during hot, dry weather. It works on your skin in much the same way, locking in moisture.

TLC Cuticle Oil

If your cuticles need a little extra tender loving care, hook them up with this nourishing oil. The sweet-smelling blend of jojoba and herbal essential oils will make them stronger and healthier in no time.

Best for:

♥ All skin types, especially ▲ Dry

TOP TIP: If you have damaged or dry cuticles, apply this oil at least two or three times a day. If you have healthy cuticles, apply this oil once or twice a day to maintain them.

- Glass bottle with lid

½ cup	jojoba oil	125 mL
12	drops peppermint essential oil (see Did you know?, page 123)	12
8	drops lavender essential oil (see Did you know?, opposite)	8

1. Pour jojoba oil, peppermint essential oil and lavender essential oil into bottle. Shake vigorously until well combined.

2. Shake bottle to recombine before each use. Massage a small amount all over nails before bed, paying special attention to cuticles.

3. Store at room temperature for up to 6 months.

DID YOU KNOW?
Jojoba oil has a long shelf life — you can keep a bottle of it for up to three years. It doesn't contain triglycerides like other vegetable oils (such as grapeseed or coconut), so it doesn't oxidize or turn rancid easily.

Lavender Hand Sanitizer

Sanitize and de-germify your hands while you relax to the calming floral aroma of lavender. This sanitizer is so handy (pun intended) when you find yourself without access to soap and water. I keep a stash of it in my house, my car and my purse at all times.

Best for:

♥ All skin types

★ Superstar ingredient:

Aloe vera gel is an ultra-fab moisturizer. In this formula, it keeps the alcohol in the witch hazel from drying out your skin.

• *Plastic squeeze bottle*

½ cup	aloe vera gel	125 mL
1½ tsp	witch hazel (see Superstar ingredient, page 242)	7 mL
⅛ tsp	vitamin E oil (see Did you know?, page 214)	0.5 mL
5 to 10	drops lavender essential oil	5 to 10

1. In a small bowl, stir aloe vera gel with witch hazel until well combined.

2. Stir in vitamin E oil and lavender essential oil. Spoon into bottle.

3. Squirt a small amount of sanitizer on palms. Rub all over hands, making sure to get between fingers, until dry. If you can, use a nail brush with it, too.

4. Store at room temperature for up to 2 months.

DID YOU KNOW?

Lavender has been used for thousands of years to wash and purify the skin; the Ancient Greeks, Romans and Persians all loved it. It is naturally antiseptic, antifungal, antibacterial and antimicrobial.

Appendices
and
Resources

Appendices

Appendix A: Favorite Natural, Organic Ingredients
and What They Do 252

Appendix B: Favorite All-Natural,
Vegan-Friendly Beauty Brands 254

Appendix C: DIY Beauty Routines:
Looking Gorgeous from Morning to Night 258

Appendix D: Tips for Labeling, Packaging
and Giving DIY Vegan Beauty Products 261

Resources

The Best Places to Shop for Ingredients,
Tools and Supplies 262

Resources for Vegan Living and Vegan Beauty 264

Appendix A: Favorite Natural, Organic Ingredients and What They Do

Here's a quick guide to many of my favorite ingredients in this book and the roles they play in my recipes. You'll find more info on these and other plant-based ingredients and essential oils — and the vitamins, minerals and nutrients they contain — in Chapter 3 (page 39) and highlighted throughout the recipes:

Aloe vera gel: Moisturizes, acts as an anti-inflammatory and antiseptic agent, helps fight acne

Argan oil: Absorbs quickly into skin, fights wrinkles, helps prevent stretch marks

Arrowroot powder: Thickens and stabilizes mixtures, helps skin absorb moisture

Avocado oil: Acts as an exceptional moisturizer and emollient, softens skin, treats symptoms of eczema and psoriasis, improves skin elasticity, penetrates skin well, has natural SPF

Baking soda: Fights odor, acts as an anti-inflammatory agent

Bentonite clay: Acts as an antibacterial agent, removes excess oil, helps remove impurities from pores

Candelilla wax: Emulsifies and thickens mixtures

Cane sugar: Exfoliates skin, is rich in natural enzymes

Castile soap: Cleanses using plant-based oils, is good for skin and hair; I love Dr. Bronner's organic Baby Unscented Pure-Castile Liquid Soap (visit www.lisabronner.com/dilutions-cheat-sheet-for-dr-bronners-castile-soap for tons of uses for this soap, such as washing dishes, doing laundry and all-purpose cleaning, scrubbing fruits and veggies, and even giving Fido a bath)

Castor oil: Acts as an antiviral, antibacterial and antifungal agent; helps treat a variety of skin conditions; reduces pain; stimulates the immune system

Chamomile essential oil: Acts as an anti-inflammatory agent, calms and soothes skin irritations

Cider vinegar: Cleanses and restores skin, balances pH

Cocoa butter: Softens; moisturizes; has a sweet, chocolaty scent

Coconut oil: Is rich in antioxidants, acts as an antimicrobial agent, moisturizes, has natural SPF

Grapeseed oil: Acts as an astringent, is rich in antioxidants that are more potent than vitamins C and E

Green tea: Acts as an antioxidant, anti-inflammatory, astringent and antibacterial agent; helps reduce puffiness and enlarged pores

Hemp seed oil: Moisturizes, acts as an anti-inflammatory agent, helps stimulate skin cell growth

Jojoba oil: Moisturizes, absorbs quickly into skin without feeling heavy, balances oil production because it is similar to skin's natural sebum, fights wrinkles and scars, has natural SPF

Lavender essential oil: Acts as an antiseptic, antibacterial and antifungal agent

Olive oil: Moisturizes

Peppermint essential oil: Acts as an anti-inflammatory, antibacterial, antifungal and antiseptic agent; cools and soothes

Rolled oats, finely ground: Soothe skin irritations, act as an anti-inflammatory agent, exfoliate, soften skin, reduce inflammation, absorb excess oil

Rose essential oil: Acts as an antibacterial, anti-inflammatory and antiseptic agent; disinfects; hydrates; fights acne

Rose hip seed oil: Fights signs of aging, acts as an anti-inflammatory agent, moisturizes

Sea salt: Acts as an antibacterial agent, exfoliates, contains a wide array of minerals and trace elements

Shea butter: Acts as an emollient, hydrates deeply, acts as an antimicrobial agent

Sweet almond oil: Moisturizes well because it is similar to skin's natural sebum, acts as an anti-inflammatory agent, fights itching and soreness, treats symptoms of eczema particularly well

Sweet orange essential oil: Acts as an astringent and antifungal agent, fights acne

Tea tree essential oil: Acts as an antifungal, antiseptic, antimicrobial and antibacterial agent; fights acne and odors

Vanilla (extract, absolute and powder): Contains antioxidants, acts as an aphrodisiac and anti-inflammatory agent, improves mood, calms

Vitamin E oil: Promotes healing, reduces the appearance of scars

Witch hazel: Acts as a mild antibacterial agent and astringent, shrinks enlarged pores, cleanses, fights acne

APPENDIX B: FAVORITE ALL-NATURAL, VEGAN-FRIENDLY BEAUTY BRANDS

While I know you'll love making beauty products from scratch, there will be times when you will want to splurge on fancy store-bought goodies. I'm a beauty blogger, so I'd be lying if I told you I use only handmade cosmetics. But the good news is that there are tons of vegan-friendly, cruelty-free brands that pride themselves on embracing an all-natural, nontoxic philosophy. Here's a list of beauty brands (and the products they offer) that I think are helping pave the way for a chemical-free future. I've reviewed most of these brands on my website, www.veganbeautyreview.com, so check it out for even more info.

Brand	Makeup	Skin Care	Hair Care	Natural Hair Dyes	Sunscreens
100% Pure	●	●	●		●
Acure Organics		●	●		
Alba Botanica		●	●		
Antonym	●				
Au Naturale Cosmetics	●				
Aubrey Organics		●	●	●	●
Bare Bones Body Care*		●			
Blue Labelle*		●	●		
Booda Organics*		●			
Coola					●
derma E*		●	●		●
Desert Essence		●	●		
DeVita*	●	●			
Earthly Body*	●	●	●		
Earthwise Beauty		●			
Ellovi*		●			
EO Products		●	●		
Everyday Minerals	●				
Everyday Shea			●		
EVOLVh			●		
Fairy Girl	●				
FitGlow Beauty	●	●			

Brand	Makeup	Skin Care	Hair Care	Natural Hair Dyes	Sunscreens
Gabriel Cosmetics, Inc.	●	●			
Giovanni			●		
Herbatint				●	
The Honest Co.		●	●		●
Hugo Naturals*		●	●		
Indie Lee		●			
Jane Carter Solution			●		
Jane Iredale	●	●			
Jāsön		●	●		●
Jersey Shore Cosmetics*	●	●			●
Juice Beauty	●	●			
Just the Goods*	●	●	●		
Kiss My Face		●	●		●
Kypris		●			
Lavanila		●			●
Lily Lolo	●				
MAHALO Skin Care		●			
Marie Veronique Advanced		●			
Meow Meow Tweet*		●			
Mineral Fusion	●	●	●		
Modern Minerals	●				
Monave Minerals	●				
Morrocco Method			●	●	
MuLondon*		●			
MyChelle Dermaceuticals		●			●
Nature's Gate*		●	●		●
Naturtint				●	
Neuma			●		
Nevo			●		
nyl Skincare*		●			

Brand	Makeup	Skin Care	Hair Care	Natural Hair Dyes	Sunscreens
Original Sprout*			•		•
OSEA Malibu*		•			
Pacifica*	•	•			
Pelle Beauty*		•			
Raw Gaia*		•			
Red Apple Girls	•				
Root Science*		•			
Safe Harbor Natural Suncare					•
Sante Naturkosmetik	•	•	•	•	
Shea Moisture	•	•	•	•	
Strawberry Hedgehog*		•			
Sunevenus			•		
Suntegrity Skincare					•
Tata Harper	•	•			
Thesis Beauty		•			
Trader Joe's		•	•		
The Wonder Seed*		•	•		
Youngblood Mineral Cosmetics	•				
Zabana Essentials		•	•		

NOTE: Companies marked with an asterisk (*) sell only 100% vegan products.

A Couple of Notes on Hair Color

First off, henna is a great, all-natural alternative to synthetic hair dye. Use it if you love color without chemicals.

Second, full disclosure: my hair has been pink — bright pink! — on and off since 1995. Is that color natural? No, it's not, and this is a constant source of struggle for me. Every choice you (and I) make can't be 100% natural all the time. But I do have a smart tip if you absolutely *must* bleach your hair before dyeing it or use a dye product that contains potentially toxic ingredients. Try to avoid applying it directly to your scalp. You may have a little line of your natural color peeking through, but you'll decrease your exposure to toxins, which is always a good choice.

Nail Polish

The good stuff in this category can be tough to find. Always read labels when you're shopping for nail polish, and keep an eye out for the following toxic and/or nasty ingredients: animal ingredients, camphor, dibutyl phthalate (DBP) and other phthalates, formaldehyde (and formaldehyde resin), fragrances, parabens, toluene, triphenyl phosphate (TPHP) and xylene.

Luckily, there are a number of brands you can trust. Some better-for-you polishes are labeled *5-free,* which means they don't contain five of the worst additives: camphor, DBP, formaldehyde, formaldehyde resin and toluene. There are also other formulas (labeled 7- or even *10-free*), which omit even more nasties, such as fragrances, parabens, phthalates and xylene. I recommend 100% Pure, AILA, ella + mila, Joshik, LVX, Pacifica, Priti, Trust Fund Beauty and Zoya.

There are also some good water-based nail polishes, which use water instead of solvents as their base. They also tend to avoid synthetic FD&C dyes, which is fabulous. Just make sure you confirm which shades are vegan before you order. Certain colors — especially reds — may contain carmine (crushed beetles — yech). Brands I recommend are 1143 H2O Nail Polish, Acquarella, Honeybee Gardens, Piggy Paint and Suncoat.

Appendix C: DIY Beauty Routines: Looking Gorgeous from Morning to Night

Life is colorful, unpredictable and wonderful, and often it pulls you in many different directions at once. Some days, you have all the time in the world to be leisurely, spa it up at home and binge-watch TV shows. Other days, you're scrambling to squeeze a bazillion to-dos into a single 14-hour window. Here's some good news: whether you're rushing out the door, heading to the gym or winding down for the night, this book has beauty recipes that'll help you look and feel amazing in the time you have available.

10-Minute Makeup

Calling all snooze button aficionados! If you find yourself constantly rushing out the door with little to no time to paint your face, I gotcha, boo. Here is an all-natural, easy-peasy beauty-enhancing makeup routine that will have you gorgeous and ready to go in 10 minutes:

1. **Apply foundation:** Flawless Powder Foundation (page 202) or Luminous Liquid Foundation (page 201)

2. **Add blush:** Shimmer Blush (page 208)

3. **Swipe on mascara:** All-Natural Vegan Mascara (page 214)

4. **Add lip color:** Tinted Lip Balm (page 222)

Post-Gym Beauty Routine

Need a fuss-free, quick beauty routine to follow after a sweaty gym sesh? These refreshing beauty must-haves will restore your babe-ness and make the most of that healthy glow:

1. **Slap on deodorant:** Keep-It-Dry Deodorant Paste (page 232) or Baking Soda–Free Spray Deodorant (page 229)

2. **Use some dry shampoo:** Lavender Mint No-Poo (page 192)

3. **Add some scent:** Uniquely You Essential Oil Perfume (page 168), Take Me Away Essential Oil Perfume (page 166) or Fruity and Floral Vanilla Perfume (page 167)

4. **Dust with powder:** Vanilla Dusting Powder (page 231)

Morning Routine

Establishing a good morning skin-care routine can do wonders for your complexion. Try these simple skin-care essentials to make sure your face stays gorgeous, glowing, sexy and smooth. Where there's a selection of recipes below, choose the one that best suits your skin type:

1. **Cleanse:** Gentle Rose Water Cleanser (page 69), Simple Castile Soap Cleansers (page 70), Basic Oil Cleansers (page 72), Acne-Away Cleanser (page 73) or Forever Young Antiaging Cleanser (page 68)

2. **Tone:** Basic Toner for All Skin Types (page 75), Rose Water Toner for Dry or Sensitive Skin (page 80), Toner for Acne-Prone Skin (page 78), Gentle Antiaging Toner (page 83) or Pore-Shrinking Basil Toner (page 76)

3. **Apply serum:** Potent Antiaging Rose Serum (page 87) or Kick-Ass Wake-Up Coffee Serum (page 90)

4. **Moisturize:** Creamy Dreamy Rooibos Moisturizer (page 92)

5. **Finish with BB cream:** Beauty Balm Cream with SPF 20 (page 204)

Evening Routine

A healthy, effective evening skin-care routine is important because it helps your skin cells repair and rebuild while you're peacefully zzzz'ing away. New skin cells actually grow faster while you're sleeping. Even if you're beyond butt-tired and ready to hit the hay, take just a few minutes before bed to cleanse, tone and moisturize. It'll help rejuvenate your skin and keep blemishes and fine lines at bay. Again, if there's a choice of formulas below, pick the one that's right for your skin:

1. **Cleanse:** Gentle Rose Water Cleanser (page 69), Simple Castile Soap Cleansers (page 70), Basic Oil Cleansers (page 72), Acne-Away Cleanser (page 73) or Forever Young Antiaging Cleanser (page 68)

2. **Tone:** Basic Toner for All Skin Types (page 75), Rose Water Toner for Dry or Sensitive Skin (page 80), Toner for Acne-Prone Skin (page 78), Gentle Antiaging Toner (page 83) or Pore-Shrinking Basil Toner (page 76)

3. **Moisturize:** Creamy Dreamy Rooibos Moisturizer (page 92), Miracle Antiaging Night Cream (page 91) or Customizable Hemp Seed Facial Oil (page 88)

4. **Apply serum:** Potent Antiaging Rose Serum (page 87)

Spa Night

With all of the stresses of everyday life, it's important to unplug, unwind and treat yourself to an at-home spa date. Enjoy a little TLC with these simple and relaxing goodies — you deserve some totally Zen "you time":

1. **Relax with a facial mask:** Matcha Green Goddess Facial Mask (page 103), Green Clay Detox Facial Mask (page 106), Black Forest Chocolate Cake Facial Mask (page 104), Skin-Quenching Facial Mask (page 107), Zit-Blasting Bananarama Facial Mask (page 110), Mellow (Yellow) Out Your Skin Turmeric Facial Mask (page 108), Party Like It's 1999 Antiaging Facial Mask (page 111), Avocado Banana Skin-Soothing Smoothie Facial Mask (page 112), Antioxidant Blueberry Delight Smoothie Facial Mask (page 115) or Just-Glow-with-It Spinach Smoothie Facial Mask (page 116)

2. **Enjoy a body scrub:** Awesome Aloe Vera Body Scrub (page 140), Vanilla Latte Body Scrub (page 145), Almond Sugar Body Scrub (page 142), Holiday Pumpkin Pie Body Scrub (page 148), Flaxseed Body Scrub (page 150), Sugar Cookie Body Scrub (page 151), Coffee Body Scrub (page 146) or Sea Salt Body Scrub (page 147)

3. **Soak your tootsies:** Refreshing Footloose Soak (page 129)

Travel Essentials

My favorite toiletries for travel include time-saving and budget-friendly multipurpose items. I also always carry anti-germ spritzies, because catching a cold on vacay is the absolute worst:

1. **Lip balm:** Luscious Lip Balm (page 219); you can also use this as a hair tamer and intense moisturizer for elbows, knuckles or heels

2. **Coconut oil:** No recipe needed; just use it as a body moisturizer, hand cream and shaving cream (see box, page 42, for more on this wonder ingredient)

3. **Hand sanitizer:** Lavender Hand Sanitizer (page 249)

4. **Sunscreen:** Sunny's Homemade Sunscreen (page 118)

5. **Bug spray:** Lemon Eucalyptus and Citronella Bug Repellent (page 245)

Appendix D: Tips for Labeling, Packaging and Giving DIY Vegan Beauty Products

OK, so you've made all of these scrumptious body butters, face creams, perfumes and so on — the whole shebang. Now comes the even more fun part: preparing them for gifting. There's no right or wrong way to glamify your swanky handmade goods. The key is to have fun and (as Madonna circa 1989 would say) express yourself, hey hey! Here are a few tips and tricks to take your gifts to the next level.

Opt for Glass and Tins over Plastic

Glass has an elegant vibe, and it's an eco-friendly alternative to plastic. (Did you know that it takes *at least* 450 years for a plastic bottle to completely biodegrade?) The sweet deal with glass jars and tins is that you can reuse 'em, recycle 'em and repurpose 'em. They can be almost anything, from planters to candle holders to makeup brush holders to whatever else you can imagine. Mama Earth will thank you for your creativity.

Also, many essential oils break down plastic over time. If you use glass, you won't ever have to worry about any chemicals leaching into your goodies.

Make Some Lovely Labels

Of course, you can write labels, stickers and tags out by hand, if you like. If you're like me and have the penmanship of a third grader, you might want to design and print them using your favorite software, such as Photoshop or Microsoft Word, or cool online tools, such as PicMonkey (www.picmonkey.com) or Canva (www.canva.com).

There are plenty of websites where you can pay for label-printing services. But free = squee, so here's my hot tip: there are a ton of free printable label and sticker templates you can download from the Internet. Just search "free printable labels."

There's more to a label than just the name of the product. Here are some of the other things you might want to include: the ingredients in the product, directions for use, storage deets (such as "Refrigerate after opening" or "Keep out of direct sunlight") and an expiry or a best-used-by date.

Add Some Extras and Frilly Bits

Dress up your DIY gifties and you'll bedazzle your recipients. You can add almost anything: stickers, ribbons, pretty fabric scraps, wrapping paper, tissue paper, lace, bows, twine, fresh and dried herbs and flowers, and cinnamon sticks. Don't be afraid to whip out your cutest stamps and glitter, too. Make your present scream, "I'm the best damn body scrub/moisturizer/lip balm *ever!*"

Put It in a Pretty Package

For a little extra oomph — or if you need something to store and present multiple handmade gifts in — package your treats in a reusable receptacle. Try wooden or metal gift baskets; organza, burlap or linen baggies; decorated gift boxes; holiday stockings; and mini-totes.

Resources

The Best Places to Shop for Ingredients, Tools and Supplies

Some of the recipes in this book require ingredients you already have in your kitchen, such as fruits, veggies, cooking oils and spices. However, there are recipes that will call for not-so-common household ingredients, such as jojoba oil, shea butter, candelilla wax, skin-friendly clays and essential oils. These items are easy to get online, and in health food stores and craft stores.

The Essentials

Here are some good places to look for supplies, including tools, butters, waxes and oils:

Amazon
www.amazon.com (United States)
www.amazon.ca (Canada)
www.amazon.co.uk (United Kingdom)
Offers worldwide shipping

ebay
www.ebay.com (United States)
www.ebay.ca (Canada)
www.ebay.co.uk (United Kingdom)
Offers worldwide shipping

Elements Bath and Body
www.elementsbathandbody.com
Offers worldwide shipping

G Baldwin & Co.
www.baldwins.co.uk
Offers worldwide shipping

Making Cosmetics
www.makingcosmetics.com
Offers worldwide shipping

Mountain Rose Herbs
www.mountainroseherbs.com
Offers shipping to the United States and Canada

Starwest Botanicals
www.starwest-botanicals.com
Offers shipping to the United States and Canada

TKB Trading
www.tkbtrading.com
Offers worldwide shipping

High-Quality Essential Oils

A quick note about the commonly used marketing term *therapeutic-grade* in relation to essential oils: there is no official grading system for the quality of essential oils (such as grade A, B or C) or an official designation of *therapeutic-grade*. Essential oils should be pure and unadulterated, but since these terms aren't regulated, companies can market their oils as such without having to pass any quality-control tests. When in doubt, contact the company directly and ask them how their essential oils are extracted, processed and manufactured. Here are a few fantastic essential oil brands that I commonly use:

Aura Cacia
www.auracacia.com
Offers shipping to the United States

Edens Garden
www.edensgarden.com
Offers worldwide shipping

Floracopeia
www.floracopeia.com
Offers shipping to the United States

Mountain Rose Herbs
www.mountainroseherbs.com
Offers shipping to the United States and Canada

Now Essential Oils
www.nowfoods.com
Sold internationally in health food stores

Labels and Packaging Supplies

These are the stores to visit when you're looking for labels, bottles, tins and jars:

Avery
www.avery.com
Offers worldwide shipping; you can also design and print labels online at this website

BayouSome.com
www.bayousome.com
Offers worldwide shipping

Evermine
www.evermine.com
Offers worldwide shipping

Making Cosmetics
www.makingcosmetics.com
Offers worldwide shipping

Moo
www.moo.com
Offers worldwide shipping

Online Labels, Inc.
www.onlinelabels.com
Offers worldwide shipping

SKS Bottle & Packaging, Inc.
www.sks-bottle.com
Offers worldwide shipping

Resources for
Vegan Living and Vegan Beauty

Learn more about what you can do to help animals, Mother Earth and yourself by choosing to go vegan. The resources below are great places to do some research and get started:

The Farm Sanctuary
www.farmsanctuary.org

Humane Society International
www.hsi.org

Leaping Bunny Program
www.leapingbunny.org

Mercy for Animals
www.mercyforanimals.org

One Green Planet
www.onegreenplanet.org

PETA
www.peta.com

peta2
www.peta2.com

Vegan Outreach
www.veganoutreach.org

The Vegan Society
www.vegansociety.com

VegNews Magazine
www.vegnews.com

Vegan Beauty Review

… and, of course, please visit me at **Vegan Beauty Review,** **www.veganbeautyreview.com**, or hit me up at VBR's social media hotspots:

 Instagram: @veganbeautyreview

 Facebook: www.facebook.com/veganbeautyreview

 Twitter: @vegan_beauty

 YouTube: www.youtube.com/veganbeautyreview

Sign up for my e-news blast so we can keep in touch, OK? I'll see you there!

Index

A

acne-prone skin, products for, 79
  Acne-Away Cleanser, 73
  Awesome Aloe Vera Body
    Scrub, 140
  Basic Oil Cleanser for Acne-Prone
    Skin, 72
  Flaxseed Body Scrub, 150
  Fruity Beer Face Scrub, 171
  Green Clay Detox Facial
    Mask, 106
  Invigorate-Me Body Wash, 123
  Keep-It-Dry Deodorant Paste, 232
  Matcha Green Goddess Facial
    Mask, 103
  Mellow (Yellow) Out Your Skin
    Turmeric Facial Mask, 108
  Pick-Me-Up Bath Fizzy, 132
  Pore-Shrinking Basil Toner, 76
  Simple Castile Soap Cleanser for
    Acne-Prone Skin, 70
  Toner for Acne-Prone Skin, 78
  Witch Hazel Aftershave, 242
  Zit-Blasting Bananarama
    Facial Mask, 110
  Zit-Zapping Blemish Stick, 84
  Zit-Zapping Body Wash, 127
activated charcoal
  All-Natural Vegan Mascara, 214
  Charcoal Natural Tooth
    Whitener, 235
  Queen of Egypt Eyeliner, 211
  Sparkly Queen of Egypt
    Eyeliner, 211
  Spice Girl Shadows, 217
aftershave, 242
alkanet root powder
  Matte and Shimmer Blushes, 208
  Tinted Lip Balm, 222
All-Natural Vegan Mascara, 214
almond flour, 142
  Hella-Bomb Oatmeal Facial
    Scrub, 99
almond meal, 51
almond milk
  Black Forest Chocolate Cake
    Facial Mask, 104
  DIY Almond Milk, 143
almond oil. See sweet almond oil.
almonds
  Almond Sugar Body Scrub, 142
  DIY Almond Milk, 143
aloe vera, 64, 140, 158
aloe vera gel, 82, 252
  All-Natural Vegan Mascara, 214
  Awesome Aloe Vera Body
    Scrub, 140

Beach Bunny Sea Salt Spray, 196
For Flakes' Sake Dandruff
  Shampoo, 176
Forever Young Antiaging
  Cleanser, 68
Gentle Antiaging Toner, 83
Gentle Rose Water Cleanser, 69
Lavender Hand Sanitizer, 249
No-Brainer Makeup Remover, 64
Peppermint Pow! Stimulating
  Shampoo, 174
Sparklepuss Glitter Gel, 158
aloe vera juice
  Lovely Lavender Fresh-Face
    Spray, 82
  Tea Tree Oil Leave-In
    Conditioner, 177
animal testing, 20–23, 25
antiaging products. See also mature
  skin, products for.
  Forever Young Antiaging
    Cleanser, 68
  Fruity AHA Facial Peel, 100
  Gentle Antiaging Toner, 83
  Miracle Antiaging Night
    Cream, 91
  Party Like It's 1999 Antiaging
    Facial Mask, 111
  Pore-Shrinking Basil Toner, 76
  Potent Antiaging Rose Serum, 87
Antioxidant Blueberry Delight
  Smoothie Facial Mask, 115
Aphrodite Body Wash, 126
apricot kernel oil, 41, 47
  Basic Oil Cleanser for Mature
    Skin, 72
argan oil, 41, 47, 252
  Creamy Dreamy Rooibos
    Moisturizer, 92
  Forever Young Antiaging
    Cleanser, 68
  Kick-Ass Wake-Up Coffee
    Serum, 90
  Miracle Antiaging Night
    Cream, 91
arrowroot powder, 56, 252
  Fab Finishing Powder, 206
  Flawless Powder Foundation, 202
  Keep-It-Dry Deodorant Paste, 232
  Lavender Mint No-Poo, 192
  Matte and Shimmer Blushes, 208
  Spice Girl Shadows, 217
  Sun-Kissed Bronzer, 207
  Vanilla Dusting Powder, 231
avocado oil, 41, 47, 119, 252
  Basic Oil Cleanser for
    Dry Skin, 72

For Flakes' Sake Dandruff
  Shampoo, 176
Heavenly Lotion Bars, 160
Kick-Ass Wake-Up Coffee
  Serum, 90
Lavender Luster Serum, 191
Natural Hair Lightener, 181
Potent Antiaging Rose Serum, 87
Sunny's Homemade
  Sunscreen, 118
avocados
  Avocado Banana Skin-Soothing
    Smoothie Facial Mask, 112
  Beer Conditioner, 171
  Deep Hydration Avocado Hair
    Mask, 186
  Party Like It's 1999 Antiaging
    Facial Mask, 111
Awesome Aloe Vera Body Scrub, 140

B

baking soda, 56, 252
  Basic Facial Scrub, 94
  Keep-It-Dry Deodorant Paste, 232
  Peppermint Toothpaste, 236
  Pick-Me-Up Bath Fizzy, 132
  Refresh-Your-Breath Minty
    Mouthwash, 234
  Refreshing Footloose Soak, 129
  Strawberry Natural Tooth
    Whitener, 239
  Vanilla Cupcake Bath Salts, 135
  Vanilla Dusting Powder, 231
Baking Soda–Free Spray
  Deodorant, 229
bananas, 33, 239
  Avocado Banana Skin-Soothing
    Smoothie Facial Mask, 112
  Just-Glow-with-It Spinach
    Smoothie Facial Mask, 116
  Mellow (Yellow) Out Your Skin
    Turmeric Facial Mask, 108
  Zit-Blasting Bananarama
    Facial Mask, 110
baobab seed oil, 47
base oils, 41–45, 46, 47
Basic Body Wash Base, 122
Basic Facial Scrub, 94
Basic Oil Cleanser for Acne-Prone
  Skin, 72
Basic Oil Cleanser for Dry Skin, 72
Basic Oil Cleanser for Mature
  Skin, 72
Basic Oil Cleanser for Normal
  Skin, 72
Basic Toner for All Skin Types, 75
basil essential oil, 54, 210

basil leaves
  Avocado Banana Skin-Soothing
    Smoothie Facial Mask, 112
  Pore-Shrinking Basil Toner, 76
bath and body care, 121–171
bath products. *See also* body scrubs;
  body washes.
  Beer Bubble Bath, 171
  Orange Vanilla Bubble Bath, 130
  Pick-Me-Up Bath Fizzy, 132
  Refreshing Footloose Soak, 129
  Vanilla Cupcake Bath Salts, 135
BB cream, 204
Beach Bunny Sea Salt Spray, 196
Beauty Balm Cream with
  SPF 20, 204
beauty brands, 25, 254–256
beauty routines, 62, 258–260
Bee-Sting Lip Plumper, 223
Beer Bubble Bath, 171
Beer Conditioner, 171
Beer Face Scrub, 171
Beer Shampoo, 171
beet root powder
  Lavender Mint No-Poo for
    Redheads, 192
  Matte and Shimmer Blushes, 208
  Spice Girl Shadows, 217
  Tinted Lip Balm, 222
beet sugar, 51
beets, 208
  Lip and Cheek Stain, 224
bentonite clay, 50, 252
  All-Natural Vegan Mascara, 214
bergamot essential oil, 53, 54, 55
  Fruity and Floral Vanilla
    Perfume, 167
  Sexy and Feminine Perfume, 168
BHA and BHT, 19, 28
Black Forest Chocolate Cake Facial
  Mask, 104
black pepper essential oil, 54
black tea, 180
  Crystal-Clear Rinse for
    Brunettes, 182
blemishes. *See also* acne-prone skin,
  products for.
  Zit-Zapping Blemish Stick, 84
blue chamomile essential oil, 53
blueberries
  Antioxidant Blueberry Delight
    Smoothie Facial Mask, 115
blush, 208. *See also* bronzer.
body butters, 152–154
body scrubs, 45, 140–142, 145–151
body washes, 122–127
bone char, 51, 145
borage oil, 47
brands, 25, 254–256
brittle hair, products for, 188, 191.
  See also dry hair, products for.

bronzer, 207
Brown Queen of Egypt Eyeliner, 211
brown sugar
  Almond Sugar Body Scrub, 142
  Coffee Body Scrub, 146
  Holiday Pumpkin Pie Body
    Scrub, 148
  Pore De-Gunking Coffee Facial
    Scrub, 96
  Pucker-Up Peppermint Lip
    Scrub, 66
bubble baths, 130, 171
bug repellent, 42
  Lemon Eucalyptus and
    Citronella Bug Repellent, 245

C

calendula oil, 47
candelilla wax, 49, 56, 252
  Beauty Balm Cream with
    SPF 20, 204
  Creamy Dreamy Rooibos
    Moisturizer, 92
  Go-Go Jojoba Solid Perfume, 164
  Heavenly Lotion Bars, 160
  Luscious Lip Balm, 219
  Miracle Antiaging Night
    Cream, 91
  Shea Butter Lipstick, 220
  Sunny's Homemade
    Sunscreen, 118
  Sweet Almond Hand Cream, 246
  Tinted Lip Balm, 222
  Zit-Zapping Blemish Stick, 84
cane sugar, 252
carnauba wax, 49
carrier oils, 41–45, 46, 47, 56
carrot seed essential oil, 53, 119
  Customizable Hemp Seed
    Facial Oil, 88
  Sunny's Homemade Sunscreen, 118
castile soap, 56, 252
  Acne-Away Cleanser, 73
  Basic Body Wash Base, 122
  Beer Bubble Bath, 171
  For Flakes' Sake Dandruff
    Shampoo, 176
  Makeup Brush Cleaner, 200
  Orange Vanilla Bubble Bath, 130
  Peppermint Pow! Stimulating
    Shampoo, 174
  Simple Castile Soap Cleansers, 70
castor oil, 41, 46, 47, 212, 252
  Almond Oil Lash-Growth
    Serum, 213
  Basic Oil Cleansers, 72
  Cedarwood Essential Oil
    Hair-Growth Treatment, 188
  Zit-Blasting Bananarama
    Facial Mask, 110
  Zit-Zapping Blemish Stick, 84

cedarwood essential oil, 191
  Cedarwood Essential Oil
    Hair-Growth Treatment, 188
  Earthy and Peaceful Perfume, 168
  Woodland Mystic Perfume, 166
cellulite, products for, 146
chamomile essential oil, 52, 252. *See
  also* blue chamomile essential oil;
  German chamomile essential oil;
  Roman chamomile essential oil.
  Coconut-Shea Smooth-Shave
    Cream, 240
  Oh My Sore Muscles! Oil, 139
chamomile tea
  Gentle Antiaging Toner, 83
charcoal. *See* activated charcoal.
Chocolate Orange Whipped
  Body Butter, 154
cider vinegar, 56, 79, 252
  Cider Vinegar Hair Rehab
    Rinses, 180
  Crystal-Clear Rinse for
    Brunettes, 182
  Tangle Wrangler, 185
  Toner for Acne-Prone Skin, 78
cinnamon
  Beauty Balm Cream with
    SPF 20, 204
  Fab Finishing Powder, 206
  Fall Pumpkin Deep-Moisturizing
    Body Treatment, 163
  Flawless Powder Foundation, 202
  Holiday Pumpkin Pie Body
    Scrub, 148
  Lavender Mint No-Poo for
    Redheads, 192
  Spice Girl Shadows, 217
cinnamon essential oil, 53, 54, 206
  Bee-Sting Lip Plumper, 223
citric acid powder
  Pick-Me-Up Bath Fizzy, 132
citronella essential oil
  Lemon Eucalyptus and
    Citronella Bug Repellent, 245
Clarifying Lemon Rinse, 181
clary sage essential oil, 54, 210
  Cider Vinegar Hair Rehab
    Rinse, 180
  Gentle Antiaging Toner, 83
  Lovely Lavender and Sage
    Conditioner, 178
  Moisturizing Makeup
    Remover, 65
  Zen Body Wash, 124
clay, 50
  All-Natural Vegan Mascara, 214
  Basic Facial Scrub, 94
  Black Forest Chocolate Cake
    Facial Mask, 104
  Green Clay Detox Facial
    Mask, 106

Hella-Bomb Oatmeal Facial Scrub, 99
Keep-It-Dry Deodorant Paste, 232
Lavender Mint No-Poo, 192
cleansers, 62, 68–73
clove bud essential oil
Oh My Sore Muscles! Oil, 139
clove essential oil, 52, 53, 54
coal tar dyes, 28
cocoa butter, 47, 49, 56, 252
Chocolate Orange Whipped Body Butter, 154
Easy-Peasy Two-Ingredient Body Butter, 152
Heavenly Lotion Bars, 160
Preggo-Essential Stretch Mark–Prevention Cream, 170
Shea Butter Lipstick, 220
Zit-Zapping Blemish Stick, 84
cocoa essential oil
Cupcake in a Bottle Perfume, 166
cocoa powder
Beauty Balm Cream with SPF 20, 204
Black Forest Chocolate Cake Facial Mask, 104
Brown Queen of Egypt Eyeliner, 211
Fab Finishing Powder, 206
Flawless Powder Foundation, 202
Lavender Mint No-Poo for Brunettes, 192
Matte and Shimmer Blushes, 208
Skin-Quenching Facial Mask, 107
Spice Girl Shadows, 217
Sun-Kissed Bronzer, 207
coconut milk
For Flakes' Sake Dandruff Shampoo, 176
Lovely Lavender and Sage Conditioner, 178
coconut oil, 41, 42–43, 47, 56, 57, 119
Awesome Aloe Vera Body Scrub, 140
Chocolate Orange Whipped Body Butter, 154
Coconut-Shea Smooth-Shave Cream, 240
Coffee Body Scrub, 146
Easy-Peasy Two-Ingredient Body Butter, 152
Fall Pumpkin Deep-Moisturizing Body Treatment, 163
Flaxseed Body Scrub, 150
Keep-It-Dry Deodorant Paste, 232
Lip and Cheek Stain, 224
Luminous Liquid Foundation, 201
Oh My Sore Muscles! Oil, 139
Preggo-Essential Stretch Mark–Prevention Cream, 170

Sunny's Homemade Sunscreen, 118
Sweet Almond Hand Cream, 246
Vanilla Latte Body Scrub, 145
coconut water
Lovely Lavender Fresh-Face Spray, 82
coffee
Coffee Body Scrub, 146
Kick-Ass Wake-Up Coffee Serum, 90
Pore De-Gunking Coffee Facial Scrub, 96
Vanilla Latte Body Scrub, 145
combination skin, products for
Coconut-Shea Smooth-Shave Cream, 240
Green Clay Detox Facial Mask, 106
Keep-It-Dry Deodorant Paste, 232
Lip and Cheek Stain, 224
Matcha Green Goddess Facial Mask, 103
Mellow (Yellow) Out Your Skin Turmeric Facial Mask, 108
Witch Hazel Aftershave, 242
comedogenic ratings, 47
conditioners, 171, 177, 178
corn oil, 47
cornmeal
Not-So-Basic Facial Scrub, 95
cornstarch, 56
Keep-It-Dry Deodorant Paste, 232
Lavender Mint No-Poo, 192
cotton seed oil, 47
Creamy Dreamy Rooibos Moisturizer, 92
Crystal-Clear Rinse for Brunettes, 182
Customizable Hemp Seed Facial Oil, 88
cuticles, products for, 248
cypress essential oil, 54
Simple Castile Soap Cleanser for Mature Skin, 70

D

dandruff-prone hair, products for
Beach Bunny Sea Salt Spray, 196
Cedarwood Essential Oil Hair-Growth Treatment, 188
Cider Vinegar Hair Rehab Rinse for Dandruff-Prone Hair, 180
Clarifying Lemon Rinse, 181
For Flakes' Sake Dandruff Shampoo, 176
Lovely Lavender and Sage Conditioner, 178
Dead Sea salt, 51
Beach Bunny Sea Salt Spray, 196
Deep Hydration Avocado Hair Mask, 186

deodorant, 228, 229, 232. *See also* dusting powder.
dibutyl phthalate (DBP), 28, 257
diethanolamine (DEA), 19, 28
DIY Almond Milk, 143
DMDM hydantoin, 28
dry hair, products for, 45
Cedarwood Essential Oil Hair-Growth Treatment, 188
Cider Vinegar Hair Rehab Rinse for Dry Hair, 180
Clarifying Lemon Rinse, 181
Deep Hydration Avocado Hair Mask, 186
Lavender Luster Serum, 191
Lovely Lavender and Sage Conditioner, 178
Peppermint Pow! Stimulating Shampoo, 174
Rosemary Mint Anti-Frizz Serum, 189
Tangle Wrangler, 185
dry lips, products for, 66, 219–222
dry shampoo, 192
dry skin, products for
Aphrodite Body Wash, 126
Awesome Aloe Vera Body Scrub, 140
Basic Oil Cleanser for Dry Skin, 72
Coconut-Shea Smooth-Shave Cream, 240
Fall Pumpkin Deep-Moisturizing Body Treatment, 163
Flaxseed Body Scrub, 150
Forever Young Antiaging Cleanser, 68
Gentle Rose Water Cleanser, 69
Keep-It-Dry Deodorant Paste, 232
Lip and Cheek Stain, 224
Lock-It-In Makeup Setting Spray, 218
Luminous Liquid Foundation, 201
Moisturizing Makeup Remover, 65
Party Like It's 1999 Antiaging Facial Mask, 111
Rose Water Toner for Dry or Sensitive Skin, 80
Simple Castile Soap Cleanser for Dry Skin, 70
Skin-Quenching Facial Mask, 107
Sweet Almond Hand Cream, 246
TLC Cuticle Oil, 248
dusting powder, 231

E

Easy-Peasy Two-Ingredient Body Butter, 152

Epsom salt, 51
 Pick-Me-Up Bath Fizzy, 132
 Refreshing Footloose Soak, 129
 Vanilla Cupcake Bath Salts, 135
essential oils, 52–54
eucalyptus essential oil, 52, 53, 54
 Cider Vinegar Hair Rehab Rinse
 for Dandruff-Prone Hair, 180
evening primrose essential oil, 47, 52
exfoliants, 51
eyelashes, products for, 213, 214
eyeliners, 211
eyeshadows, 217

F

Fab Finishing Powder, 206
face care, 61–119
facial masks, 33, 50, 62, 103–116
facial oil, 88
facial peel, 100
facial scrubs, 51, 62, 94–99, 171.
 See also lip scrub.
Fall Pumpkin Deep-Moisturizing
 Body Treatment, 163
Farm Sanctuary, 18
feet, products for, 129, 231
fennel essential oil, 54
finishing powder, 206
Flawless Powder Foundation, 202
flax seeds
 Flaxseed Body Scrub, 150
 Flaxseed Hair-Styling Goop, 194
flaxseed oil, 194
 Beer Conditioner, 171
Floral and Romantic Perfume, 168
For Flakes' Sake Dandruff
 Shampoo, 176
Forever Young Antiaging
 Cleanser, 68
formaldehyde, 19, 28, 257
foundations, 201–204
fragrance, 30
frankincense essential oil, 52, 53,
 54, 210
 Customizable Hemp Seed
 Facial Oil, 88
 Moisturizing Makeup
 Remover, 65
 Potent Antiaging Rose Serum, 87
 Simple Castile Soap Cleanser for
 Mature Skin, 70
French green clay, 50
 Basic Facial Scrub, 94
 Green Clay Detox Facial
 Mask, 106
frizzy hair, products for, 42, 45,
 177, 189
Fruity AHA Facial Peel, 100
Fruity and Floral Massage Oil, 136
Fruity and Floral Vanilla
 Perfume, 167

Fruity Beer Face Scrub, 171
fuller's earth clay, 50
 Basic Facial Scrub, 94

G

garlic, 79
Gentle Antiaging Toner, 83
Gentle Rose Water Cleanser, 69
geranium essential oil, 54, 210
 Basic Toner for All Skin Types, 75
 Customizable Hemp Seed
 Facial Oil, 88
 Floral and Romantic Perfume, 168
German chamomile essential oil, 54
ginger essential oil, 54
glycerin. *See* vegetable glycerin.
Go-Go Jojoba Solid Perfume, 164
granulated sugar
 Flaxseed Body Scrub, 150
 Hair Spray-bilizer, 197
 Sugar Cookie Body Scrub, 151
 Vanilla Latte Body Scrub, 145
grapefruit essential oil, 52, 53, 54, 153
 Beach Bunny Sea Salt Spray, 196
 Fruity and Floral Massage
 Oil, 136
 Young and Flirty Perfume, 168
grapefruit seed extract, 57
grapeseed oil, 41, 47, 56, 191, 253
 Awesome Aloe Vera Body
 Scrub, 140
 Customizable Hemp Seed
 Facial Oil, 88
 Party Like It's 1999 Antiaging
 Facial Mask, 111
 Sea Salt Body Scrub, 147
 Take Me Away Essential Oil
 Perfume, 166
Green Clay Detox Facial Mask, 106
green tea, 56, 253
 Cider Vinegar Hair Rehab
 Rinses, 180
 Toner for Acne-Prone Skin, 78
guar gum
 Lovely Lavender and Sage
 Conditioner, 178
gums, products for, 234–239

H

hair care, 42, 171, 173–197
hair dye, 28, 31, 256
hair mask, 186
Hair Spray-bilizer, 197
hand cream, 246
hand sanitizer, 249
hazelnut oil, 47, 119
 Basic Oil Cleanser for Acne-Prone
 Skin, 72
Heavenly Lotion Bars, 160
Hella-Bomb Oatmeal Facial
 Scrub, 99

hemp seed oil, 44, 47, 253
 Customizable Hemp Seed
 Facial Oil, 88
 Just-Glow-with-It Spinach
 Smoothie Facial Mask, 116
henna, 256
hibiscus flower powder
 Lavender Mint No-Poo for
 Redheads, 192
 Matte and Shimmer Blushes, 208
 Spice Girl Shadows, 217
highlighter, 201
 Sparkly Illuminating Cream, 210
Himalayan pink salt, 51
 Vanilla Cupcake Bath Salts, 135
Holiday Pumpkin Pie Body
 Scrub, 148
honeybees, 160
hydroquinone, 28

I

illuminating cream, 210
imidazolidinyl urea, 28
infusing carrier oils, 46
ingredient labels, 20, 28–31, 257
insect repellent. *See* bug repellent.
Invigorate-Me Body Wash, 123

J

jasmine essential oil, 52, 53, 54
 Aphrodite Body Wash, 126
 Sexy and Feminine Perfume, 168
 Simple Castile Soap Cleanser for
 Dry Skin, 70
jojoba oil, 44, 45, 47, 56, 119, 253
 Awesome Aloe Vera Body
 Scrub, 140
 Basic Oil Cleanser for Normal
 Skin, 72
 Beauty Balm Cream with
 SPF 20, 204
 Bee-Sting Lip Plumper, 223
 Coconut-Shea Smooth-Shave
 Cream, 240
 Coffee Body Scrub, 146
 Customizable Hemp Seed
 Facial Oil, 88
 Flaxseed Body Scrub, 150
 Go-Go Jojoba Solid Perfume, 164
 Lavender Luster Serum, 191
 Lemon Eucalyptus and Citronella
 Bug Repellent, 245
 Luminous Liquid Foundation,
 201
 Makeup Brush Cleaner, 200
 Moisturizing Makeup
 Remover, 65
 No-Brainer Makeup Remover, 64
 Rosemary Mint Anti-Frizz
 Serum, 189
 Sweet Almond Hand Cream, 246

Take Me Away Essential Oil
Perfume, 166
TLC Cuticle Oil, 248
juniper berry essential oil, 53, 54
Woodland Mystic Perfume, 166
Just-Glow-with-It Spinach Smoothie
Facial Mask, 116

K

kaolin clay, 50
Basic Facial Scrub, 94
Black Forest Chocolate Cake
Facial Mask, 104
Keep-It-Dry Deodorant Paste, 232
Lavender Mint No-Poo, 192
Keep-It-Dry Deodorant Paste, 232
Kick-Ass Wake-Up Coffee
Serum, 90
kokum butter, 49

L

lavender essential oil, 52, 53, 54, 153,
210, 253
Aphrodite Body Wash, 126
Chamomile and Lavender
Sleepytime Lotion, 159
For Flakes' Sake Dandruff
Shampoo, 176
Fruity and Floral Massage
Oil, 136
Fruity and Floral Vanilla
Perfume, 167
Invigorate-Me Body Wash, 123
Lavender Hand Sanitizer, 249
Lavender Luster Serum, 191
Lavender Mint No-Poo, 192
Lemon Eucalyptus and Citronella
Bug Repellent, 245
Lovely Lavender and Sage
Conditioner, 178
Lovely Lavender Fresh-Face
Spray, 82
Peppermint Pow! Stimulating
Shampoo, 174
Simple Castile Soap Cleanser for
Dry Skin, 70
Sun-Kissed Bronzer, 207
Sweet Almond Hand Cream, 246
Tangle Wrangler, 185
TLC Cuticle Oil, 248
Zen Body Wash, 124
lead, 28, 220
lemon essential oil, 52, 53, 153
Cider Vinegar Hair Rehab Rinse
for Oily Hair, 180
Customizable Hemp Seed
Facial Oil, 88
Fruity and Floral Vanilla
Perfume, 167
Hella-Bomb Oatmeal Facial
Scrub, 99

Pick-Me-Up Bath Fizzy, 132
Simple Castile Soap Cleanser
for Acne-Prone Skin, 70
Unicorn Kisses Shimmer
Lotion, 156
Zit-Zapping Body Wash, 127
lemon eucalyptus essential oil
Lemon Eucalyptus and Citronella
Bug Repellent, 245
lemongrass essential oil, 53, 54, 210
Cider Vinegar Hair Rehab Rinse
for Oily Hair, 180
lime essential oil, 153
Lip and Cheek Stain, 224
lip balms, 219, 222, 223
lip scrub, 66
lipstick, 220
Lock-It-In Makeup Setting
Spray, 218
lotions, 156, 159, 160
Lovely Lavender and Sage
Conditioner, 178
Lovely Lavender Fresh-Face
Spray, 82
Luminous Liquid Foundation, 201
Luscious Lip Balm, 219

M

macadamia nut oil, 119
makeup and cosmetics, 199–225
Makeup Brush Cleaner, 200
makeup removers, 42, 45, 64, 65
mango butter, 49
Beauty Balm Cream with
SPF 20, 204
maple syrup
Pore De-Gunking Coffee Facial
Scrub, 96
marula oil
Forever Young Antiaging
Cleanser, 68
Miracle Antiaging Night
Cream, 91
mascara, 214
massage oils, 42, 45, 136, 139
Matcha Green Goddess Facial
Mask, 103
Matte Blush, 208
mature skin, products for
Antioxidant Blueberry Delight
Smoothie Facial Mask, 115
Basic Oil Cleanser for Mature
Skin, 72
Coconut-Shea Smooth-Shave
Cream, 240
Customizable Hemp Seed
Facial Oil, 88
Forever Young Antiaging
Cleanser, 68
Gentle Antiaging Toner, 83
Gentle Rose Water Cleanser, 69

Keep-It-Dry Deodorant
Paste, 232
Lip and Cheek Stain, 224
Luminous Liquid Foundation,
201
Mellow (Yellow) Out Your Skin
Turmeric Facial Mask, 108
Miracle Antiaging Night
Cream, 91
Party Like It's 1999 Antiaging
Facial Mask, 111
Pore-Shrinking Basil Toner, 76
Potent Antiaging Rose Serum, 87
Simple Castile Soap Cleanser
for Mature Skin, 70
measuring ingredients, 39, 40
Mellow (Yellow) Out Your Skin
Turmeric Facial Mask, 108
methylisothiazolinone, 28
mica powder
Shea Butter Lipstick, 220
Shimmer Blush, 208
Sparklepuss Glitter Gel, 158
Sparkly Illuminating Cream, 210
Sparkly Queen of Egypt
Eyeliner, 211
Unicorn Kisses Shimmer
Lotion, 156
Vanilla Dusting Powder, 231
Miracle Antiaging Night Cream, 91
moisturizers. *See also* body butters.
Beauty Balm Cream with
SPF 20, 204
Creamy Dreamy Rooibos
Moisturizer, 92
Customizable Hemp Seed
Facial Oil, 88
Miracle Antiaging Night
Cream, 91
Moisturizing Makeup Remover, 65
mouthwash, 234
myrrh essential oil, 52, 53
Cider Vinegar Hair Rehab Rinse
for Dry Hair, 180
Simple Castile Soap Cleanser
for Mature Skin, 70

N

nail polish, 257
nails, products for, 248
nanoparticles, 28
neroli essential oil, 54, 210
night cream, 91
No-Brainer Makeup Remover, 64
normal skin, products for
Basic Oil Cleanser for Normal
Skin, 72
Coconut-Shea Smooth Shave
Cream, 240
Green Clay Detox Facial
Mask, 106

Keep-It-Dry Deodorant
Paste, 232
Lip and Cheek Stain, 224
Luminous Liquid Foundation,
201
Matcha Green Goddess Facial
Mask, 103
Mellow (Yellow) Out Your Skin
Turmeric Facial Mask, 108
Witch Hazel Aftershave, 242
Not-So-Basic Facial Scrub, 95
nutmeg
Beauty Balm Cream with
SPF 20, 204
Flawless Powder Foundation, 202
Spice Girl Shadows, 217
nutmeg essential oil, 54

O
Oh My Sore Muscles! Oil, 139
oily hair, products for, 180, 196
oily skin, products for, 156
Acne-Away Cleanser, 73
Awesome Aloe Vera Body
Scrub, 140
Flaxseed Body Scrub, 150
Green Clay Detox Facial
Mask, 106
Invigorate-Me Body Wash, 123
Keep-It-Dry Deodorant Paste, 232
Matcha Green Goddess Facial
Mask, 103
Mellow (Yellow) Out Your Skin
Turmeric Facial Mask, 108
Pick-Me-Up Bath Fizzy, 132
Pore-Shrinking Basil Toner, 76
Simple Castile Soap Cleanser
for Acne-Prone Skin, 70
Toner for Acne-Prone Skin, 78
Witch Hazel Aftershave, 242
Zit-Blasting Bananarama
Facial Mask, 110
Zit-Zapping Blemish Stick, 84
Zit-Zapping Body Wash, 127
olive oil, 44, 47, 56, 119, 253
Awesome Aloe Vera Body
Scrub, 140
Coffee Body Scrub, 146
Deep Hydration Avocado
Hair Mask, 186
Flaxseed Body Scrub, 150
Makeup Brush Cleaner, 200
Shea Butter Lipstick, 220
Skin-Quenching Facial Mask, 107
orange essential oil. See sweet
orange essential oil; wild orange
essential oil.
oregano essential oil, 52
organic foods, 35–36
organic ingredients, 252–253
oxybenzone, 30

P
packaging beauty products, 261, 263
palmarosa essential oil
Floral and Romantic Perfume, 168
papayas
Fruity AHA Facial Peel, 100
paprika (sweet)
Spice Girl Shadows, 217
parabens, 30
parfum (fragrance), 30
Party Like It's 1999 Antiaging
Facial Mask, 111
patchouli essential oil, 53
Aphrodite Body Wash, 126
peppermint essential oil, 52, 53, 54,
153, 253
Cider Vinegar Hair Rehab Rinse
for Dry Hair, 180
Invigorate-Me Body Wash, 123
Lavender Mint No-Poo, 192
Luscious Lip Balm, 219
Peppermint Pow! Stimulating
Shampoo, 174
Peppermint Toothpaste, 236
Pick-Me-Up Bath Fizzy, 132
Pucker-Up Peppermint
Lip Scrub, 66
Refresh-Your-Breath Minty
Mouthwash, 234
Refreshing Footloose Soak, 129
Rosemary Mint Anti-Frizz
Serum, 189
Shea Butter Lipstick, 220
Simple Castile Soap Cleanser
for Acne-Prone Skin, 70
TLC Cuticle Oil, 248
Unicorn Kisses Shimmer
Lotion, 156
Witch Hazel Aftershave, 242
Zit-Zapping Blemish Stick, 84
perfumes, 164–168
petroleum by-products, 30
phthalates, 30
Pick-Me-Up Bath Fizzy, 132
pimples. See acne-prone skin,
products for.
pineapple
Fruity AHA Facial Peel, 100
plant butters, 47, 49
polyethylene glycol, 30
pomegranate oil, 47
Pore De-Gunking Coffee Facial
Scrub, 96
Pore-Shrinking Basil Toner, 76
Potent Antiaging Rose Serum, 87
pregnancy, 30, 54, 55
Preggo-Essential Stretch Mark–
Prevention Cream, 170
product labels, 20, 28–31, 257
propylene glycol, 30
Pucker-Up Peppermint Lip Scrub, 66

pumpkin purée
Fall Pumpkin Deep-Moisturizing
Body Treatment, 163
Holiday Pumpkin Pie Body
Scrub, 148
pumpkin seed oil, 47

Q
Queen of Egypt Eyeliner, 211

R
red raspberry seed oil, 119
Sunny's Homemade
Sunscreen, 118
Refresh-Your-Breath Minty
Mouthwash, 234
Refreshing Footloose Soak, 129
resorcinol, 31
rhassoul clay, 50
Basic Facial Scrub, 94
Hella-Bomb Oatmeal Facial
Scrub, 99
Lavender Mint No-Poo for
Redheads, 192
rice bran oil, 119
rice flour
Vanilla Dusting Powder, 231
rinses, 180–182
rolled oats, 51, 253
Basic Facial Scrub, 94
Hella-Bomb Oatmeal Facial
Scrub, 99
Not-So-Basic Facial Scrub, 95
Skin-Quenching Facial Mask, 107
Roman chamomile essential oil
Chamomile and Lavender
Sleepytime Lotion, 159
Zit-Zapping Body Wash, 127
rooibos tea leaves
Creamy Dreamy Rooibos
Moisturizer, 92
Kick-Ass Wake-Up Coffee
Serum, 90
rose essential oil, 52, 53, 54, 253
Potent Antiaging Rose Serum, 87
Sexy and Feminine Perfume, 168
rose geranium essential oil
Floral and Romantic Perfume, 168
Young and Flirty Perfume, 168
rose hip seed oil, 44, 46, 47, 52, 253
Miracle Antiaging Night
Cream, 91
rose petals
Rose Water Toner for Dry or
Sensitive Skin, 80
rose water
Basic Toner for All Skin Types, 75
Gentle Rose Water Cleanser, 69
rosemary essential oil, 52, 53, 54, 191
Customizable Hemp Seed
Facial Oil, 88

Earthy and Peaceful Perfume, 168
Invigorate-Me Body Wash, 123
Miracle Antiaging Night
    Cream, 91
Refreshing Footloose Soak, 129
Rosemary Mint Anti-Frizz
    Serum, 189
Sun-Kissed Bronzer, 207
Witch Hazel Aftershave, 242
rosemary oil extract, 57
rosewood essential oil
    Floral and Romantic Perfume, 168

S

safflower oil, 47
sage essential oil, 53, 54. *See also*
    clary sage essential oil.
sage leaves
    Crystal-Clear Rinse for
        Brunettes, 182
salts, 51, 56. *See also* Epsom salt;
    sea salt.
    Vanilla Cupcake Bath Salts, 135
sandalwood essential oil, 53, 153
    Aphrodite Body Wash, 126
    Sexy and Feminine Perfume, 168
    Zen Body Wash, 124
sea buckthorn oil, 47
sea salt, 51, 253
    Awesome Aloe Vera Body
        Scrub, 140
    Beach Bunny Sea Salt Spray, 196
    Peppermint Toothpaste, 236
    Sea Salt Body Scrub, 147
    Vanilla Cupcake Bath Salts, 135
sensitive skin, products for
    All-Natural Vegan Mascara, 214
    Baking Soda–Free Spray
        Deodorant, 229
    Coconut-Shea Smooth-Shave
        Cream, 240
    Flaxseed Body Scrub, 150
    Gentle Rose Water Cleanser, 69
    Lock-It-In Makeup Setting
        Spray, 218
    Luminous Liquid Foundation,
        201
    Queen of Egypt Eyeliner, 211
    Rose Water Toner for Dry or
        Sensitive Skin, 80
serums, 62
    Almond Oil Lash-Growth
        Serum, 213
    Kick-Ass Wake-Up Coffee
        Serum, 90
    Lavender Luster Serum, 191
    Potent Antiaging Rose Serum, 87
    Rosemary Mint Anti-Frizz
        Serum, 189
sesame oil, 47
Sexy and Feminine Perfume, 168

shampoos, 171, 174, 176. *See also*
    dry shampoo.
shaving cream, 240
shea butter, 47, 49, 56, 253
    Beauty Balm Cream with
        SPF 20, 204
    Coconut-Shea Smooth-Shave
        Cream, 240
    Heavenly Lotion Bars, 160
    Luscious Lip Balm, 219
    Miracle Antiaging Night
        Cream, 91
    Preggo-Essential Stretch Mark–
        Prevention Cream, 170
    Shea Butter Lipstick, 220
    Spice Girl Shadows, 217
    Sunny's Homemade
        Sunscreen, 118
Shimmer Blush, 208
siloxanes, 19, 31
Simple Castile Soap Cleanser
    for Acne-Prone Skin, 70
Simple Castile Soap Cleanser
    for Dry Skin, 70
Simple Castile Soap Cleanser
    for Mature Skin, 70
Skin-Quenching Facial Mask, 107
sodium laureth and sodium lauryl
    sulfates, 19, 31
soy wax, 49
soybean oil, 47, 119
Sparklepuss Glitter Gel, 158
Sparkly Illuminating Cream, 210
Sparkly Queen of Egypt Eyeliner, 211
spearmint essential oil, 53, 54
Spice Girl Shadows, 217
spinach
    Just-Glow-with-It Spinach
        Smoothie Facial Mask, 116
spirulina powder
    Spice Girl Shadows, 217
stevia, 234
    Peppermint Toothpaste, 236
storing homemade beauty products,
    57, 261
strawberries
    Fruity Beer Face Scrub, 171
    Strawberry Natural Tooth
        Whitener, 239
sugar, 51, 56, 197. *See also* brown
    sugar; granulated sugar.
Sugar Cookie Body Scrub, 151
Sun-Kissed Bronzer, 207
sunflower oil, 44, 47
    Basic Oil Cleansers, 72
Sunny's Homemade Sunscreen, 118
sunscreens, 118, 119, 204
sweet almond oil, 44, 47, 56, 119, 253
    Almond Oil Lash-Growth
        Serum, 213
    Almond Sugar Body Scrub, 142

Awesome Aloe Vera Body
    Scrub, 140
Basic Body Wash Base, 122
Bee-Sting Lip Plumper, 223
Creamy Dreamy Rooibos
    Moisturizer, 92
Flaxseed Body Scrub, 150
Fruity and Floral Massage
    Oil, 136
Kick-Ass Wake-Up Coffee
    Serum, 90
Not-So-Basic Facial Scrub, 95
Sugar Cookie Body Scrub, 151
Sweet Almond Hand Cream, 246
Take Me Away Essential Oil
    Perfume, 166
Uniquely You Essential Oil
    Perfume, 168
sweet orange essential oil, 52, 53, 54,
    229, 253
    Aphrodite Body Wash, 126
    Beach Bunny Sea Salt Spray, 196
    Chocolate Orange Whipped
        Body Butter, 154
    Earthy and Peaceful Perfume, 168
    Luscious Lip Balm, 219
    Orange Vanilla Bubble Bath, 130
    Simple Castile Soap Cleanser
        for Acne-Prone Skin, 70
    Unicorn Kisses Shimmer
        Lotion, 156
sweet paprika
    Spice Girl Shadows, 217

T

Take Me Away Essential Oil
    Perfume, 166
tamanu oil, 47
tangerine essential oil, 53, 54
Tangle Wrangler, 185
tea tree essential oil, 52, 53, 54, 253
    Acne-Away Cleanser, 73
    Cider Vinegar Hair Rehab
        Rinse for Oily Hair, 180
    For Flakes' Sake Dandruff
        Shampoo, 176
    Simple Castile Soap Cleanser
        for Acne-Prone Skin, 70
    Tea Tree Oil Leave-In
        Conditioner, 177
    Zit-Zapping Blemish Stick, 84
    Zit-Zapping Body Wash, 127
teeth, products for, 234–239
thinning hair, products for, 188, 191
thyme essential oil, 53, 191
Tinted Lip Balm, 222
TLC Cuticle Oil, 248
toners, 62, 75–78, 80, 83
tools and supplies, 39–40, 262–263
tooth whiteners, 235, 239
toothpaste, 236

triclocarban and triclosan, 31
triethanolamine (TEA), 28
turmeric
    Matcha Green Goddess Facial
       Mask, 103
    Mellow (Yellow) Out Your Skin
       Turmeric Facial Mask, 108
    Spice Girl Shadows, 217
    Zit-Blasting Bananarama Facial
       Mask, 110

U

Unicorn Kisses Shimmer Lotion, 156
Uniquely You Essential Oil
    Perfume, 168
unisex beauty essentials, 227–249

V

vanilla absolute, 253
    Cupcake in a Bottle Perfume, 166
    Kick-Ass Wake-Up Coffee
       Serum, 90
    Vanilla Cupcake Bath Salts, 135
vanilla essential oil, 53
vanilla extract, 253
    Cupcake in a Bottle Perfume, 166
    Fruity and Floral Vanilla
       Perfume, 167
    Pucker-Up Peppermint Lip
       Scrub, 66
vanilla powder, 253
    Orange Vanilla Bubble Bath, 130
    Sugar Cookie Body Scrub, 151
    Vanilla Dusting Powder, 231
    Vanilla Latte Body Scrub, 145
Vegan Beauty Review, 10
vegan sugars, 51. *See also* brown
    sugar; granulated sugar.
vegetable glycerin
    Basic Body Wash Base, 122
    Forever Young Antiaging
       Cleanser, 68
    Fruity and Floral Vanilla
       Perfume, 167
    Gentle Rose Water Cleanser, 69
    Lock-It-In Makeup Setting
       Spray, 218

Orange Vanilla Bubble Bath, 130
Tea Tree Oil Leave-In
    Conditioner, 177
Witch Hazel Aftershave, 242
vegetable waxes, 49
vetiver essential oil, 153
vitamin A palmitate oil, 47
vitamin E oil, 47, 56, 57, 253
    Almond Oil Lash-Growth
       Serum, 213
    Chocolate Orange Whipped
       Body Butter, 154
    Creamy Dreamy Rooibos
       Moisturizer, 92
    Flaxseed Hair-Styling
       Goop, 194
    Fruity and Floral Massage
       Oil, 136
    Kick-Ass Wake-Up Coffee
       Serum, 90
    Lemon Eucalyptus and
       Citronella Bug Repellent, 245
    Luminous Liquid Foundation,
       201
    Party Like It's 1999 Antiaging
       Facial Mask, 111
    Preggo-Essential Stretch Mark–
       Prevention Cream, 170
    Tea Tree Oil Leave-In
       Conditioner, 177
    Zit-Zapping Blemish Stick, 84

W

wheat germ oil, 47, 119
white kaolin clay. *See* kaolin clay.
white rice flour
    Vanilla Dusting Powder, 231
wild orange essential oil, 153
wintergreen essential oil, 54, 153
    Oh My Sore Muscles! Oil, 139
witch hazel, 56, 79, 253
    Baking Soda–Free Spray
       Deodorant, 229
    Fruity and Floral Vanilla
       Perfume, 167
    Gentle Rose Water Cleanser, 69
    Lavender Hand Sanitizer, 249

Lemon Eucalyptus and
    Citronella Bug Repellent, 245
Refresh-Your-Breath Minty
    Mouthwash, 234
Witch Hazel Aftershave, 242
Woodland Mystic Perfume, 166

X

xylitol powder
    Refresh-Your-Breath Minty
       Mouthwash, 234

Y

ylang-ylang essential oil, 52, 53,
    54, 210
    Aphrodite Body Wash, 126
    Cupcake in a Bottle Perfume, 166
    Floral and Romantic
       Perfume, 168
    Simple Castile Soap Cleanser
       for Dry Skin, 70
    Woodland Mystic Perfume, 166
    Young and Flirty Perfume, 168
yogurt
    Antioxidant Blueberry Delight
       Smoothie Facial Mask, 115
    Avocado Banana Skin-Soothing
       Smoothie Facial Mask, 112
    Green Clay Detox Facial
       Mask, 106
    Mellow (Yellow) Out Your Skin
       Turmeric Facial Mask, 108
    Young and Flirty Perfume, 168

Z

Zen Body Wash, 124
zinc oxide
    Beauty Balm Cream with
       SPF 20, 204
    Sunny's Homemade
       Sunscreen, 118
zits, products for. *See also* acne-prone
    skin, products for.
    Zit-Blasting Bananarama Facial
       Mask, 110
    Zit-Zapping Blemish Stick, 84
    Zit-Zapping Body Wash, 127

Library and Archives Canada Cataloguing in Publication

Subramanian, Sunny, author
    The compassionate chick's guide to DIY beauty : 125 recipes for vegan, gluten-free, cruelty-free makeup,
skin & hair products / Sunny Subramanian of veganbeautyreview.com & Chrystle Fiedler.

Includes index.
ISBN 978-0-7788-0547-2 (paperback)

    1. Beauty, Personal. 2. Cosmetics. 3. Natural products. 4. Hair—Care and hygiene. 5. Skin—Care and
hygiene. 6. Sustainable living. I. Fiedler, Chrystle, author II. Title.

RA776.98.S83 2016   646.7'2   C2016-902416-4